Soviet Princeton

SOVIET
PRINCETON

Slim Evans and the 1932–33 Miners' Strike

Jon Bartlett Rika Ruebsaat

NEW STAR BOOKS
VANCOUVER
2015

New Star Books Ltd.
#107–3477 Commercial Street | Vancouver, B.C. V5N 4E8 canada
1574 Gulf Road, #1517 | Point Roberts, WA 98281 usa
NewStarBooks.com | info@NewStarBooks.com

The publisher acknowledges the financial support of the Canada Council for the Arts, the Government of Canada through the Canada Book Fund, the British Columbia Arts Council, and the Province of British Columbia through the Book Publishing Tax Credit.

Cataloguing information for this book is available from Library and Archives Canada, www.collectionscanada.gc.ca.

Cover design by Oliver McPartlin (McPartlin.ca)
Interior design by New Star Books
Printed & bound in Canada on 100% post-consumer recycled paper by Imprimerie Gauvin, Gatineau, QC
First printing, November 2015

isbn: 978-1-55420-109-9 (print), 978-1-55420-110-5 (epub)

Contents

Preface

THE IDEA FOR this book came from a photograph and two songs. We first came across the photograph you see on page 65 in *Princeton Our Valley*, one of those large vanity press jobs which include everyone's reminiscences of the Jones's place or the old mill out at Five Mile. The cutline for the photo read, "a prank." The editors either didn't know, or didn't want to know, who "Evanskivitch" was or what his "dupes" were up to.

The songs were collected by Phil Thomas in a couple of visits to Princeton in 1974. "The cops'll have a hell of a time / Trying to break the picket line" was one (though the informant recited the words, rather than singing it to "Inky Pinky Parlez Vous," the tune it belongs to). The second song describes in harsh verse a couple of mine bosses, but there's little about a strike. On asking around, we found some folk who knew it was connected to a baton charge by mounted policemen, and a KKK cross burning. The story obviously needed telling, and this we hope is that story.

We were materially assisted by the knowledgeable and gracious help from institutional staff at the Princeton & District Museum & Archives; the Special Collections department of the Vancouver Public Library; Rare Books & Special Collections at the University of British Columbia in Vancouver; the British

Columbia Archives at the Royal B.C. Museum in Victoria; and the National Library & Archives in Ottawa. Dr. Stephen Endicott was especially generous with his guide to relevant documents. We thank, too, Anna & Paul Bjarnason, Marne St. Clair, and John Schreiber for their hospitality and guidance.

In small towns such as Princeton, there is often knowledge which is "secret" or shared among a few people. Sometimes it means that A hasn't spoken to any member of B's family since 1947, when . . . you can draft the plot in your own mind. Often libellous, never actually complete, such knowledge can poison the atmosphere between new and old residents of the town. We suspect that there are memories in our town which will be dislodged on reading this book, and perhaps the memories will not be pleasant ones. For that reason, we have not included in the book any oral histories: our sources are all public documents, either the presses (pro and con), court documents, or specialist books. Our thanks to all those townsfolk who helped us on our quest: but the interpretation of what these documents report, of course, is ours, and ours alone.

Jon Bartlett & Rika Ruebsaat
Princeton, September 2015

ONE

PRINCETON, 1932

PRINCETON'S HISTORY REFLECTS its location in British Columbia, midway between Vancouver and the Okanagan: the town was once a supply centre for ranchers, and then became a resource extraction town, with the local mines and logging/milling operations providing the town's livelihood. The miners owned no land and often no houses, and were thus often regarded by the ranching interests as rootless and alien, with no interest in the town or its well-being.[1] Over the years, as large-scale mining operations continued, Princeton was the scene of several industrial strikes and lockouts, both in the coal industry of the 1930s as well as in the copper mining industry of the 1940s. This legacy has helped give Princeton its reputation as a tough town with a fractious history.

This is the story of a heated confrontation that took place in Princeton during the depths of the Great Depression—a struggle over coal mine owners' attempts to roll back miners' wages. It's a dramatic story that features mounted police charging a picket line; searches of workers' houses for subversive literature; physical assaults; the creation of a Citizens' League to oppose the miners' union; a kidnapping; crosses burning in the hills above town; the editor of the local paper, Dave Taylor, rallying opposition to the miners (the archives of the *Princeton Star* are one of the best sources of information about these events); and the conviction of the strike leader, Arthur "Slim" Evans, for advocating the overthrow of the government by force.

✳

Long before Europeans entered the landscape, local First Nations knew the site as a source of red ochre, hence the early name, Vermilion Forks. Princeton received its current name and its first survey in 1860, when it was a collection of shacks serving the needs of a few ranchers, notably John Fall Allison. These earliest Anglo-European settlers recognized in the "bunchgrass country" a fine site to run cattle, which could then be shipped to the growing Lower Mainland.

Although Allison noted the presence of copper and coal in the area, large-scale mining was not deemed commercially viable until the turn of the century. In the meantime miners came to the area for gold and platinum. A gold rush at nearby Granite Creek in 1885 resulted in a boomtown reputed to be for a few years the third-largest settlement in B.C.

The 1891 Census lists 220 people in the Princeton area.[2] This figure would have included people living in what is now the town of Princeton, but most would have lived at Granite Creek, some nineteen kilometres away, the only established settlement in the region.[3] Fully one third were Chinese men and another quarter were First Nations people. Another quarter were born in Canada. Those who were neither First Nations nor Chinese comprised twenty-six females and sixty-four males, a gender imbalance which still obtained in the 1921 census. Most of the men were placer miners, working the Tulameen River and its creeks following the big Granite Creek gold rush of 1885. Those who were not miners were, as it were, support staff—cooks, storekeepers and their clerks, and farmers and farm labourers.

In 1898 the Waterman brothers, through their Vermilion Forks Mining and Development Company, bought the twelve-hundred-acre townsite from Allison's son-in-law, and in the years that followed, laid out and sold lots.[4] The brothers bought the land from a man who had married into the extensive Allison clan, and Ernest Waterman became, once the brothers had acquired British financial backers, a resident director, and in 1903, a Justice of the Peace. Each issue of the local paper carried a full-page advertisement for the land company. Waterman co-founded Princeton Light & Power in 1922, and was Secretary of the local hospital for many years.

After the 1885 gold rush copper provided the next excitement. One day in 1884 a trapper named James Jameson discovered copper ore while hunting deer near Princeton. His discovery led to a rush of miners to the area and eventually gave rise to the settlement of Copper Mountain, about ten kilometres south of Princeton. The first camps located in the area were "Volcanic" Brown's Camp and E. Voight's Camp, which soon merged to create the Granby Company's Copper Mountain operation. Mining at Copper Mountain began tentatively with the first shipment in October 1920; almost immediately the mine closed on a slump in the price of copper, and remained inactive until 1925. In 1926, as global copper prices rose, the mine was reopened and 138 men were hired. Two years later there were 370 workers (255 underground miners, 121 surface workers) at Copper Mountain, and by 1930 B.C.'s minister of mines noted "fully 500 men." But Copper Mountain mine closed in 1931, and did not reopen until 1937.[5]

Gold and copper were relative flashes in the pan compared to coal, which spurred the main mining activity in Princeton from 1905 onward. The Princeton coal basin extends twenty-four kilometres in length by four to seven kilometres in breadth, and over the course of some forty years it engendered at least ten coal mines in and around Princeton. By 1910 coal mining was clearly the predominant industry in the region, and already by the 1921 Census one quarter of all workers in the town described themselves as miners or coal miners. Many of the rest were employed as labourers in the coal mines, and together with all the ancillary trades of haulage, carpentry, and administration, it was clear to all that coal mining was the lifeblood of the town.

The first functioning coal mine was owned by the Vermilion Forks Mining and Development Company. It first shipped a few tons of coal in 1909, but by 1925 it was played out. Its peak year was 1917, when it shipped over forty-six thousand tons and employed sixty-six workers.

Though a mine named the United Empire Colliery shipped some coal in 1912 and 1913, nothing further is heard of it, and it was not until 1924 that Princeton had its second coal mine. It was owned by Tulameen Coal Mines Ltd., and was popularly known as the Tulameen mine, or "Charlie Hunter's mine." This mine was at the centre of the disturbances in 1932–33.

Charlie Hunter had a ranch about 2.5 kilometres west of Princeton, reachable by a wagon road that followed the north bank of the Tulameen River. It was on this road that he discovered an outcropping of coal in 1924. He set to work with his partner Ben Bowen to exploit the find, and by the end of the year had ten men working on it. That year saw the production of just over one thousand tons of coal; the next year production increased to 6,851 tons, with twenty-two miners employed. In 1929 the owners built a spur to the Princeton–Tulameen line of the Kettle Valley Railway and production increased steadily, peaking at around fifty thousand tons between 1931 and 1933, with around 120 to 140 men working in the mine.[6]

Princeton's population is stated as one thousand in the 1932 edition of the *Directory*, a boosterish annual published in Vancouver by Sun Directories, an offshoot of the daily newspaper. The town was served by two railways: the Vancouver, Victoria & Eastern, a branch line of the Great Northern; and the Kettle Valley Railway, a subsidiary of the Canadian Pacific Railway. The VV&E from Republic, Washington crossed the U.S. border near Chopaka and made its way up the Similkameen valley, through Keremeos and Hedley, on its way to Princeton. The KVR was routed from Penticton through Summerland, and then down through the hills to Princeton, the junction of the two railways. A single track headed up the Tulameen River to Brookmere, where it met the CPR Coquihalla route from Merritt to Hope, the route now taken by the Coquihalla Highway.

There was a gravel road that followed the north bank of the Similkameen east from Princeton to Hedley and Keremeos, and another road northwest to Coalmont and Tulameen, and then on to Merritt. The Hope–Princeton Highway, though partially navigable at the time, would only be completed after the Second World War.

The 1932 *Directory* listed some 445 names, of which 193 (some 43 percent) were identified as miners, three-quarters of whom worked for the Tulameen mine. The balance worked in the six cafes, two hotels, four garages, four churches, two banks, and twenty-four shops and stores listed in the *Directory*. Thirty-two townspeople were farmers, ranchers or dairymen; fourteen worked in the trades, a dozen in the local schools, and another dozen for the provincial government in one capacity or another. There was the Princeton Brewery, a bowling alley, a billiards room and a theatre. Ten people worked for the B.C. Telephone Co., and ten for the two railways. Others worked for a power company and a waterworks company, four were agents for oil companies, and three were listed as insurance agents. There were branches or lodges of the Canadian Legion, the Oddfellows, the Masons, the Order of the Eastern Star and the Daughters of Rebekah. There was the *Princeton Star* newspaper, and an undertaker. We can picture Princeton's population as a mix of mainly English, Scottish or American settlers, with a large minority, perhaps a third, from eastern Europe, many of them working in the mines.[7]

The Similkameen and the Tulameen rivers meet at Princeton, where a ridge of high ground divides them. Because the railway station and its associated wye—a railway loop to allow engines, in the absence of a turntable, to turn around—were alongside the Similkameen, and the route north followed the Tulameen, a tunnel was bored through this ridge. It was in this area of town, the low-lying flats alongside the railway right-of-way, known as "The Tunnel," that many of these eastern Europeans lived, and where the first meeting of miners would take place.

✳

The events in Princeton of 1932–33 occurred in the midst of the Great Depression, as it was long characterized. The economic crisis of the 1930s was widely regarded at the time as the most dangerous capitalism had ever met. Many thought that capitalism had reached its final crisis.

The depression of 1929–1937 was neither the first nor the last of its kind, but it was certainly great by any standard. Wall Street's Dow Jones index of the value of traded stocks fell from its 1929 peak of 381.17 to only 41.22 by early July of 1932. It would not reach that 1929 peak again until 1955. The financial collapse was followed by a collapse in industrial production, which was followed in turn by a collapse of industrial trade. The only growth in sight was that of unemployment; in the depths of the depression in Canada, this reached 27 percent. This misery was accompanied and exacerbated in the west of North America by several years of drought, wherein farmers reaped the whirlwind of the foolish agricultural techniques of the preceding generation.

To those in power, the remedy was obvious. "Liquidate," treasury secretary Andrew Mellon advised President Hoover:

> Liquidate labor, liquidate stocks, liquidate farmers, liquidate real estate . . . it will purge the rottenness out of the system. High costs of living and high living will come down. People will work harder, live a more moral life. Values will be adjusted, and enterprising people will pick up the wrecks from less competent people.[8]

Capitalism was seen as a natural phenomenon, and the natural remedy presented itself—after overeating, purge oneself. Old, inefficient businesses collapsed so that new enterprises could grow, in much the same way that a forest fire, though terrible and destructive, allows new growth to reach the sunlight.

This doctrine, shared by the dominant mainstream electoral parties in Canada, the Conservatives and Liberals, was anathema to a growing proportion of those who had borne the brunt of the economic depression—propertyless workers with nothing to sell but their labour power. To them, the depression was nothing short of catastrophic. Hundreds of thousands of Canadians took to the roads and railways, looking for work.

Perhaps this was the beginning of the end for capitalism—but did it have to be this way? Was it natural for the system to suddenly stop working? Many looked to government for a solution within the capitalist system; many others looked beyond the present form of governance to a new kind of system. For them, history was unfolding exactly as Marx had predicted decades earlier, when he claimed the working class would grow in numbers and organizational strength, and the expropriators would eventually, and inevitably, be expropriated. Capitalism was destroying itself through its own internal contradictions, and the working class would be its gravedigger. But a new society was in the making in the U.S.S.R. Many visitors came back from the new socialist workers' paradise echoing the famous declaration of the American journalist Lincoln Steffens, who declared, upon returning from a 1919 visit, "I have seen the future, and it works."

The political left was led not only by political parties, striving for success and power in the electoral realm, but more importantly, by workers' organizations at the level of their workplace and industries: unions. This organized left thought of itself as the vanguard of a working class on the threshold of taking its place in history as the midwife overseeing the birth of a new society, run by and in the interests of the vast majority whose labour made society what it was. A crucial part of this vanguard's role, its members believed, was educating less-politicized workers about the inherent contradictions of capitalism. When the depression struck they spread the good news that this was not only a disaster, but also an opportunity, and they were there to help in the day-to-day struggles of the working class against a dying system, whether with employers, landlords or the state. The enthusiasm with which the younger politicized workers took to this message was palpable, and still radiates from the pages of the leftist press, particularly the *Unemployed Worker*, and from the transcripts of the frequent court cases brought by the state against these "agitators."

These ideas were not new, especially in western Canada. The formation of the Industrial Workers of the World (the "Wobblies") in 1905 marked the beginning of a syndicalist strain in union matters: "The working class and the employing class have nothing in common," read the preamble to the IWW constitution, printed in every copy of the *Little Red Songbook*.[9] Though the older craft unions of the American Federation of Labor still followed the Gomperite notions of striking a bargain with capitalism, the revolutionary workers of the IWW, mostly unskilled, built trade-wide unions encompassing every worker and utterly rejected this type of deal-making. They were out to abolish, not reform, capitalism, believing it to be in its death throes.

Politically conscious workers thus fell into one of two camps: on the one hand a reformist section that strove to use government to reform or control capitalism, and on the other a revolutionary section that sought the overthrow of capitalism. The first section was represented in the 1930s by the Co-operative Commonwealth Federation (CCF); the second by the Communist Party of Canada (CPC) and its associated organizations, such as the Workers' Unity League (WUL), who declared, "The workers never got anything and never will get anything from the capitalist class unless they fight for it."[10] Without doubt, it was the second section that had the momentum, as noted by the B.C. Department of Labour in its Annual Report for 1932:

> It is a recognized fact that the majority of strikes which have occurred during the last two or three years have not been between employers and employees who belong to any of the old and estab-

lished trade unions, but have been brought about by an organization which has sprung into active being since the present abnormal conditions began, and which will disappear for lack of fertile ground, when trade conditions revive. But in the meantime it is essential for every employer and employee to endeavor to understand each other's difficulties and come together in that spirit of fair play which alone will bring a revival of business conditions.

Employers are beginning to realize that the established and recognized trade unions have been the main bulwark of safety during the last few years. There can be no doubt that had the organization which has caused many of the strikes since 1929 been able to gain control of our National and International Unions, we would have witnessed an industrial upheaval which would have shaken the foundations of established Government.

Greater co-operation between Associations of employers and 'Union officials is the only avenue by which the sinister influence at work can be held in check and finally eliminated.[11]

The Canadian Communist Party was formed in May 1921, with many of its initial members coming from such organizations as the Socialist Party of Canada, the IWW, the One Big Union, and the Socialist Labor Party. All of these groups recognized the need for propaganda work to be done among politically progressive people and at the same time in labour unions. Many of its members had been labour organizers both in Europe and in Canada and so brought to the new party a wealth of organizational experience. From its formation, the party was harassed by the RCMP—its meetings banned, its offices invaded, its documents seized, and in 1931, its leaders arrested.

But it brought to the struggle its own contradictions. Its job as it saw it was to organize, educate, and lead Canadian workers—industrial and agricultural, organized and unorganized—to overthrow capitalism and replace it with a system similar to that of the Bolshevik Party of the Soviet Union. It could thus be accused, and often was, of being an agent of a foreign power, more concerned with the welfare of the Soviet state than that of Canadian workers. It had also to confront the claim that

it predicted and advocated "the forcible overthrow of the bour-
geoisie," a phrase frequently found in both Marx and Lenin, and
was thus in breach of the strictures of section 98 of the Canadian
Criminal Code, which stated that

> Any association...whose professed purpose...is to bring about
> any governmental, industrial or economic change within Canada
> by use of force, violence or physical injury to person or property,
> or by threats of such injury, or which teaches, advocates, advises or
> defends the use of force, violence, terrorism, or physical injury to
> person or property...in order to accomplish such change, or for
> any other such purpose..., or which shall by any means prosecute
> or pursue such purpose...or shall so teach, advocate, advise or
> defend, shall be an unlawful association.

Added to these problems was the makeup of the party itself.
In 1931, as labour historian Stephen Endicott writes,

> Although the overwhelming majority of the population was made
> up of Anglo-Celtic and French-Canadian workers, 95 per cent
> of the party membership was confined to three other language
> groups — Finnish with 60 per cent, Ukrainian with 25 per cent and
> Jewish with 10 per cent. Such a national composition was a serious
> barrier between the party and the majority of workers. [12]

Princeton functioned as a supply centre for ranches in the area
but was also an industrial town with, as we have said, three-
quarters of the working population being associated with mining. The depression hit both hard, but it hit the mines the hard-
est. Writing in June 1931, M. Allerdale Grainger, a frequent visitor
to the area, noted that

> Relief or no relief, country folk showed their feeling that they can
> stand world Depression better than city people. (There's deer in
> them there hills, and milk and eggs and beef on the ranches)....
> The absence of work does not bother them.... But if you want to see
> a worried man these days, go call upon a storekeeper in a mountain

district like this where the payrolls in the mines ceased suddenly last November, with all credit accounts outstanding.[13]

The payrolls he mentions were from the Copper Mountain mine, the layoff of seven hundred men "almost bankrupting the local shops."[14] Early in 1932, owners of the Tulameen mine extracted a 10 percent pay cut from their miners, a concession which the miners were determined to get back. They talked about striking, but there was no union.

Nevertheless, the local board of trade feared that the depression would only deepen, and viewed the situation with alarm. This fear generated hysteria in its members, among them Dave Taylor, the owner and publisher of the *Princeton Star*. Princeton was "on its uppers," and these people saw the miners' talk of striking to recover their lost pay as a potential death blow. This was not an idle fear. Even then, the Canadian and U.S. west was littered with ghost towns, once-thriving communities that were abandoned when the local economic wellspring dried up.

The *Princeton Star*, of course, derived its income largely from the advertisements bought by local businesses, which had borne the brunt of the depression, perhaps even more so than the rest of the town's citizens — business owners had financial responsibilities they could not walk away from and, unlike the miners, they couldn't even leave town to look for work elsewhere, fruitless as that might have been.

The events that follow stemmed from a struggle between Princeton's mine owners and their employees, ostensibly over the refusal by the owners of one mine, the Tulameen, to fulfill their promise to restore the 10 percent pay cut they imposed on workers in April 1932.

The miners asked for and received assistance from a new revolutionary trade union centre, the Workers' Unity League, as well as from one of its constituent unions, the Mine Workers Union of Canada and its associated welfare and defence organizations. They were also assisted by a large number of the unemployed in town. The owners were assisted by Taylor and the *Star*, the town's only paper; by the local board of trade under its president, P.W. Gregory; by a vigilante organization founded by the board; by the provincial police, with some thirty officers sent to bolster the two local constables; and by the provincial courts, the government of B.C., and the federal government.

TWO

Slim Evans Comes to Princeton

HOWEVER GEOGRAPHICALLY ISOLATED Princeton may have been in 1932, its citizens were keenly aware of events unfolding in the larger world. This was the case for the workers no less so than the owners and shopkeepers — Princeton's miners were well attuned to the winds of change in the atmosphere, and the increasing attention paid to socialism. Many workers knew of the Industrial Workers of the World (commonly known in the Pacific Northwest as the Wobblies), the Communist Party, the Workers' Unity League, and other organizations springing up in different parts of the country and the world. These organizations were being established to look out for the interests of working people caught up in the depression and lead the masses to a better future. Many miners in Princeton were more than ready to throw themselves into the project of building a new world around the needs of the working class.

And so, in the fall of 1932, when the owners of the Tulameen mine refused to return the "temporary" 10 percent wage rollback imposed in the spring of that year, some Tulameen miners, who belonged to no union, took it upon themselves to invite someone from the coast to help them in their struggle. In response to their invitation the Workers' Unity League dispatched Slim Evans.

On September 13, Evans for the first time addressed a group of Tulameen miners.

★

Arthur Herbert Evans, or "Slim" Evans as he became known, was an inspiring speaker, an indefatigable union organizer, and a communist—though he denied being a capital-C Communist, i.e., a member of the Communist Party of Canada, since that was illegal.[15] His biography mirrors the political history of western North America.

Evans was born in April 1890 and raised in Toronto, where after leaving school at the age of thirteen he learned the carpenter's trade. He left Ontario in 1911 as a journeyman carpenter and headed for Winnipeg to look for work. After a few months in Manitoba and Saskatchewan, in December of that year he headed for Minneapolis, joined the Industrial Workers of the World, and was jailed for the first time.[16]

Municipal officials in the United States had begun using various public order laws to shut down labour organizers. The Wobblies took up this struggle and insisted upon their rights of association and free speech by organizing a series of "free-speech fights." Slim Evans was one of many Wobblies arrested and imprisoned for their roles in these protests.

In 1913 he travelled to Ludlow, Colorado, to take part in a miners' strike. That dispute escalated into the famous Ludlow Massacre.[17] Evans was himself wounded by machine-gun fire during the attack. After a stay in the hospital he travelled and worked throughout the northwestern states before coming back to Canada through Lethbridge, probably in 1916. He worked as a carpenter in Calgary, the Crowsnest Pass area, and Trail, B.C., and was back in Alberta in time for the founding of the One Big Union (OBU) in 1919. The OBU was a radical new union based on the principal of industrial organization, in contrast to the unionization by craft as practiced by the mainstream labour movement.

Almost immediately, Evans went to southern Alberta as organizer for the Monarch local of the OBU in the Drumheller coalfield.[18] There he was elected district secretary, and was soon front and centre in the struggle between the OBU and the established United Mine Workers of America (UMWA). The dispute was a bitter one, and was as much between the old, Gomperite UMWA and the radical new OBU as it was between the boss and the worker. In the course of the fight, Evans was accused of effectively taking over the UMWA local. With the aid of UMWA officials' testimony he was charged and convicted of fraudulent conversion for taking control of the local and its bank accounts, and in January 1924 was sentenced to three years in prison. He was released after serving fourteen months; he moved to Vancouver and joined the Carpenters' Union.

Evans joined the Communist Party of Canada (CPC) in 1926. In 1929 socialist progressives associated with the CPC founded the Workers' Unity League (WUL) as a central labour organization dedicated to fighting for workers' rights according to socialist principles. At some point Evans joined the WUL, and when the miners' call for help came in 1932 he was sent to Princeton.

He brought with him the organizing techniques of the new revolutionary unions: ceaseless struggle; frequent meetings of workers and sympathizers, with no distinction drawn between employed and unemployed; and no union bureaucracy — major decisions would all be "made from below."

Evans arrived on September 13, 1932, and met with some of the Tulameen miners at a café. They told him they wanted to recover the pay cut they had conceded in the spring. They had been assured it would be returned in September, but the owners of the Tulameen mine were reneging on their promise. The miners were now working one day a week and earning $4.50 a day.

Evans advised the miners to delay their demand. The mine was producing lignite coal, which could not be stored — when the weather turned colder, demand would increase and the mine would get back up to speed; when they were working six days a week they would be in a position of strength.

At an open-air meeting that night, Evans said the same thing to a mass rally of miners.[19] Because many of them were Yugoslavs who feared deportation, the meeting took place in the dark, in an empty lot in the Tunnel Flats. Evans later wrote "It had got so dark that no one was recognizable, so with nothing but a flash-light to read the notes with I started." He had them all sit down on the grass, since he intended to speak for ninety minutes or more. Soon, he told them, when winter came and the demand for coal increased, "I am prepared to organize a local here of the Mine Workers Union of Canada."[20]

The authorities were gearing up for trouble. The province's attorney general, Robert Pooley, ordered thirty members of the B.C. Provincial Police (ten of them mounted) and ten RCMP officers to Princeton in anticipation of a strike. "Evans is gaining a large following of miners and unemployed," wrote one B.C. Provincial Police officer. His superior wrote to the RCMP for help, saying "This man seems to be establishing himself as quite a danger, and if there is any way of removing him it would help considerably."[21] It would certainly help the mine owners.

The meaning of this large influx of police officers to their small town was not lost on the miners, who understood that the full weight of the establishment was mobilizing against them. Police testimony at Evans's subsequent section 98 trial testified to the tension and heightened anxiety caused by the large armed force, not just among workers but among many of the town's merchants and professionals.

Evans, meanwhile, had left Princeton. When he returned on 17 November a period of intense activity began, both by the miners and by the police. The miners held almost-daily meet-ings attended by two to three hundred people and addressed by Evans.[22] Miners signed up as members of the Mine Workers Union of Canada (MWUC), and the unemployed workers as members of the Canadian Labor Defense League (CLDL).

Police, as the *Princeton Star* noted ominously on 24 November, "have been giving the matter considerable attention. They have attended all the public meetings, and checked up otherwise on these activities, and have kept a record. In connection with the campaign and possibly in preparation for a possible demonstration, district authorities of the Provincial Police have been in the district this week."

A meeting of miners on 21 November was followed two days later by a "smoker," a more social affair with music, dancing, and a series of wrestling and boxing bouts. It was a rare opportunity for workers and the unemployed to get together and share their experiences over a beer.

This might also have been the impetus for the creation of the Workers' Center that was established some time before Christmas 1932 — following the incorporation of the union, it rented a hall from William H. Thomas, a Princeton old-timer who came as a carpenter (he may have built the hall himself) and was now a rancher. The hall was christened the Workers' Center, and housed meetings of miners and of the unemployed. It was also a place where workers could eat for a reasonable price, bed down if necessary, talk with fellow workers, and generally escape their social isolation amid others who lived similar lives.[23] The Workers International Relief, a sister organization of the union and the Canadian Labor Defense League, was providing food in Princeton to strikers and others, and it may well have functioned in the Workers' Center.

In the *Princeton Star* of 24 November, Dave Taylor identified Evans as a criminal: "Police state that Mr. Evans was in 1924 sentenced to three years imprisonment for embezzlement of funds of the Drumheller, Alberta, local of the United Mine Workers of America. The amount involved was $2554.27 and action was brought by the President of the Drumheller local."

Evans' response? "Let them give it all the publicity they like," he said. "The more they say about it the better I'll like it. . . . I will place all the facts before the workers on Friday evening and let them be the jury." He did just that: at a meeting the next day he drew attention to the accusation, and explained how the American Federation of Labor-affiliated UMWA had colluded with the coal bosses to rid themselves of a revolutionary opponent. "After giving his version of the incident, he was voted 'not guilty.'"[24]

This marked the beginning of the *Princeton Star*'s growing interest in Evans and the labour unrest. Over the next ten months, Dave Taylor published near-weekly articles and editorials on the matter—between 23 November 1932 and 28 September 1933 only two issues of the *Star* contained no articles or editorials on Evans or the miners' struggles. Taylor consistently portrayed Princeton as threatened by outside forces, with right-thinking, responsible citizens[25] defending their small industrial town from the alien, hate-filled agitators ranged against them.

Throughout the month the heavy police presence was the source of much tension. Soon Princeton's residents had had enough: at a mass public meeting, twenty-two merchants (out of approximately thirty in town) and several hundred workers and citizens signed a resolution calling for the withdrawal of "Pooley's Hooligans" (as they were popularly known):

> Whereas the importation of increasing numbers of provincial Police, into the town of Princeton, is primarily for the purpose of intimidating the miners who are desirous of organizing into a union to improve their rotten working conditions and low wages rates, and whereas the imported provincial Police are notorious strike breakers and thugs and who have participated in strike breaking and thuggery at Timberland and Fraser Mills strikes, and whereas in the opinions of workers and citizens of Princeton the importation of these provincial Police is wholly unnecessary, and are to be used in the cause of vested interest to keep the workers under the iron heel of the coal barons of Princeton and not in the interest of worker-taxpayers, and whereas we the workers and citizens of Princeton believe that the tax-payers money squandered in this fashion could be put to better use in the way of raising the subsistence allowance

of the unemployed therefore be it resolved that we the workers and citizens of Princeton, assembled this 25th day of November, 1932 in mass meeting numbering _____ [space left] do hereby demand the immediate withdrawal of all extra police at Princeton. Be it further resolved that the immediate cessation of the use of Provincial or other Police in any and all wage disputes. *Submitted and passed, 25th day of November 1932, Chairman of Mass Meeting, Princeton, B.C.*[26]

Much has been written about Arthur "Slim" Evans and the events of his life, but little has been written about his two adversaries in Princeton, Percy Gregory and Dave Taylor.

To start with the elder: Percy Gregory was born in England 8 June 1881, and came to Canada in 1908 at the age of twenty-seven. We know little of his training and background prior to his arrival in Princeton in or before 1918,[27] when he appears in the local directory as a land surveyor. He had at that time a wife and three children: a five-year-old, a two-year-old, and a baby born that year.

Gregory seems to have played an important role in the organizational life of Princeton. He appears in the 1919 directory as a land surveyor and a fire insurance agent, and in 1920 as the secretary of the board of trade, a position he holds (except for one year) until at least 1927, when the board of trade listing disappears. Either in that year or the next he becomes its president. In 1921 his description includes "civil engineer," and in 1927 he adds "real estate." In 1926, according to local historian Laurie Currie, he was active with Bill Ewart, the hardware merchant, in an unsuccessful campaign to incorporate the town.[28] In 1928, in addition to his surveying, insurance, and real estate business, the directory lists him as manager of British Columbian Properties Ltd., described as "Owners of Princeton Townsite and Princeton mining properties," and as the managing director of Princeton Waterworks Co. Ltd.

Dave Taylor was born 4 November 1904 in Tarbolton, Dundee, Scotland.[29] His family emigrated to Saskatchewan in 1909, and later moved to South Wellington, a coal mining community just south of Nanaimo on Vancouver Island. Taylor's father was in the grocery business. Taylor attended the University of British Columbia and joined the staff of the *Ubyssey* student newspaper. He worked there from January 1924 to his graduation in 1926, initially as a reporter and finally as sports editor under editor-in-

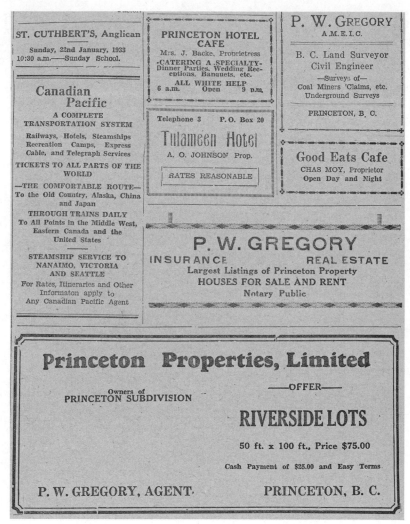

Ads for Gregory's various enterprises in Taylor's *Princeton Star* of 18 May 1933.

chief Earle Birney. After a brief stint as a reporter for Vancouver's *Province* newspaper, he arrived in Princeton in 1927 and began work for Joe Brown, the owner and editor of the *Princeton Star*. Taylor was fired following a dispute with Brown in 1929, but he offered to buy the paper and Brown accepted. Taylor stayed as proprietor and editor until 1939, when he left Princeton to go to the China.

While in Princeton he took an interest in all the sports activities on offer, and played saxophone in the town band. As the editor of the town's only paper he would have rubbed shoulders with Princeton's "great and good," and he may have appeared to his seniors as a bright young man who could be brought along. He became secretary of the board of trade for some years while Gregory was president.

As Princeton was unincorporated at the time and so had no municipal government, it was natural that an informal group of well-off and established senior men would be the ones with the loudest voices. It may well have been that Taylor, having spent only five years in Princeton, was quick to absorb the prevailing wisdom that Gregory and the other senior men imparted, wisdom he then parroted back to them in ever-more-inflammatory articles that had the solid support of the town's worthies.

We know nothing of the relationship between Taylor and Gregory in the eventful and emotional months from December 1932 to September 1933. But Taylor must have been keenly aware of the extent to which the butter on his daily bread depended upon Gregory: the *Princeton Star* was dominated by advertisements for Gregory's many and various enterprises. While this revenue could be seen as implicitly backing Taylor's increasingly hostile views, Gregory was by no means confined to the shadows—he led the kidnappers in 1933, while Taylor was apparently not present. Though there may have been disagreements on some issues (Gregory's enthusiasm for incorporation, for example), on the question of red revolutionaries and industrial strikes they stood as one.

THREE

Trouble at the Mines

AT A MEETING on Sunday, 27 November 1932, the Tulameen miners voted to form a union. The Princeton Branch (No. 20) of the Mine Workers Union of Canada was formed, with local miner H.F. Hayes as its president and John Cyprian Cherkosh as secretary. The newly unionized miners drafted a note to all the mine operators in the Princeton coal basin. It contained four demands:

1. A ten percent pay increase, effective 1st December.
4. Stoppage of all haulage for a fifteen-minute period, during change of shifts, as provided for by the Coal Mines Regulation Act.
3. Abolition of the back-hand system, and payment of back-hands at the same rate as miners.
4. Recognition of the elected pit committee and acknowledgement of their right to inspect the mine.[30]

The pay increase was merely the restoration of the pay cut imposed by the mine owners in the spring of 1932, with the promise at the time to restore it in September of that year. The second demand was a safety concern; the *Unemployed Worker*, in its 3 December issue, claimed that in the previous year three men had been killed and seventy injured at the Tulameen mine. The third issue concerned the use of back-hands, "unpapered" miners hired by the owners at $3.69 a day instead of the $4.50 that senior miners were making, a system the men wanted ended because it divided workers against each other.

The superintendent of the Tulameen mine, John Bennett, had no problem with the last demand, as long as it did not interfere with the proper functioning of the mine, but he rejected the first three demands outright. He offered as an alternative a system of contract mining, with the men paid according to how much coal they dug. This would automatically do away with the back-hand system. He said that he had always paid special attention to the safety of incoming and outgoing shifts, and that the *Coal Mines Regulation Act* did not require a fifteen-minute stoppage between shifts.

Reactions to the Tulameen miners' determination to strike varied at the two other mines operating in the basin. The Blue Flame miners decided, by a vote of twenty-five to two, not to take part in the strike. But the Pleasant Valley management, on instructions from the owner, W.R. Wilson, absolutely refused to recognize or negotiate with the union. Whether Wilson disliked this particular union or harboured antipathy to unions in general (similar to nineteenth-century Vancouver Island coal baron Robert Dunsmuir, who repeatedly refused to negotiate with any union) we do not know—although the *Star* later noted that Wilson was "satisfied that the local union is a product of the communistic regime." Nevertheless, when the Tulameen strike began the forty-five workers at the Pleasant Valley mine also came out to a man.

The strike began without incident, but the calm lasted only until the police showed up on day two. Early on the morning of Friday, 2 December, Slim Evans and other strike leaders joined about fifty picketing miners and sympathizers on the road leading to the Tulameen mine. As Corporal Cline led the police towards the striking miners, they taunted the police, reported

Workers march through the streets of Princeton, almost certainly during the 1932 strike.

the *Star*, "with many expressions, such as 'God damn hooligans' and 'thug.'" They were also treated to a song sung to the tune of "Inky Pinky Parlez-Vous," a popular (and obscene) First World War ditty. The only lines that have come down to us are "The cops are having a hell of a time / Trying to break the picket line."[31]

Patrick Driscoll, a.k.a. James Lacey (or Lacy), led the singing miners with evident enthusiasm, displaying "all the motions of the leader of a full-fledged symphony." For his efforts he was accused of "singing a song on the King's Highway," arrested and jailed for the weekend, and on the Monday appeared before the Penticton magistrate on a charge of vagrancy. The trial was reported in knockabout fashion by the *Star* in its next issue;[32] Driscoll was found guilty, fined ten dollars, and immediately filed notice of appeal.

The following day saw near-farce turn to near-tragedy in an event that is still remembered in Princeton more than eighty years later. Again the striking miners, accompanied by their wives and children and other sympathizers, formed a picket line on the road leading to the mine. Again they were confronted by the Provincial Police—but this time by eleven officers on horseback, who charged at the picket line using horses and batons ("light whips," said one of the police officers[33]) to break it up by force and chase people into the streets.

The *Star* did not report on the affair immediately, but on 8 December reported the workers' complaints, which were presented to its editor in a prepared statement read by Lacy and Sanderson, described as "representatives of the striking miners": "The police were, in the opinions of the strikers, entirely responsible for Saturday's attack." They "brutally clubbed down innocent men, women and children," and "set upon them without warning." Several men, the complaint reads, "were forced to run to the Tulameen river and swim across in its icy waters to avoid being clubbed or trampled down, and are ill as a result. Facts brought out in the trial of Comrade Lacy showed that the sympathies of the police are with the operators, and that they are here to protect the vested interests and as strike-breakers."

Evans alleged in his own trial at Vernon the following September that during the baton charge one worker's arm was broken in two places and a child was knocked unconscious. Two witnesses at the same trial testified that Constable Hatherill rode up on the sidewalk and clubbed a man talking to them.[34]

There was no immediate outcome from the fracas of 3 December, but the following Wednesday marked a watershed in the strike and the opposition to it, with several arrests made and a police raid conducted.

Early on 7 December, H.F. Hayes, president of the local union, and John Tymchuck, William Palmer, and John Beronich, executive members of the local miners and unemployed workers' associations, were charged with creating a disturbance during the skirmish between strikers and the police. (The charge against Hayes was speedily withdrawn.) A striker's wife, not named by the paper, was also arrested on the same charge: "Police gave evidence that on Monday morning, as three officers were standing in front of the Princeton Hotel on Bridge Street, the defendant came up to them and expressed her opinions of them in offensive and obscene language, and in a boisterous manner."

A more serious charge was laid against Mike Kovich, who was "alleged to have thrown a stone in Saturday's skirmish which seriously injured Constable Murphy of the B.C. police." Kovich appeared in Penticton Police Court that same day, where his case was remanded to 15 December. Bail was set at two thousand dollars, a prohibitive amount; Kovich would be jailed until his trial.

That same day, 7 December, a raid was made on the miners' headquarters, "conducted in broad daylight and without a scene," as reported by the *Star*. "Two members of the Provincial Police forced open the door and gained admittance about ten o'clock Wednesday morning. There was no one on the premises at the time."[35]

But more importantly for the overall struggle, Slim Evans was arrested the morning before[36] and charged under the infamous section 98 of the Criminal Code.[37] Evans described his arrest later in the *Unemployed Worker*: "A ton and a half of beef walked into the house at 3 a.m. Dec. 6th, six of them, and they spirited me away through back alleys so that the workers would not get wise."[38] Evans was jailed in Penticton.

Meanwhile, three directors of Tulameen Coal Mines Ltd. had arrived in Princeton, spurring rumours of a deal in the making: "Settlement within the next 24 hours of the strike," reported the *Star*, "which has tied up production in the Princeton coal field since last Wednesday was considered distinctly possible by well informed men of reasonable views, late Thursday."[39]

The union received an offer from the company on Thursday evening, to be put to a meeting of the miners on Friday, 9 December, at two p.m. The offer appears to have been for a twenty-five cent raise, which was rejected out of hand by the miners. Further discussion resulted in a new offer being made Saturday evening and ratified at the Sunday meeting of the union. The terms represented an almost complete victory for the miners: a return of the 10 percent pay cut imposed in the spring, a recognition of the union and pit committee, and fifteen minutes stoppage of all haulage in the mine on shift changeover.[40]

This was surely an occasion for the *Star* to congratulate all parties on the successful conclusion of the first act of collective bargaining in Princeton's history (and in a relatively short time, just eight days). As Taylor had written in his editorial, "Responsible," on 8 December,

> this is not a time for spite and rancour or for hot headed enthusiasm; it is rather a situation that calls for the biggest and best that is in local men; magnanimity to subjugate personal prejudice to the common good. It calls not for civil war, but for a fight that is far more difficult: a fight against personal prejudice that will pave the way to co-operation for a settlement that will be mutually advantageous, a victory that will be far greater than a mere triumph for either side.

Despite this earlier call for "magnanimity," what Taylor now proposed was closer to civil war. His issue of 15 December contained almost five thousand words about the strike, in terms of increasing vehemence. This extraordinary outpouring of vituperation was made up of hard news, background articles, and editorials. The news items, in order of decreasing size, were

- the settlement of the dispute with the Tulameen Mine;
- the refusal of the owner of the Pleasant Valley Mine to negotiate with the Union;
- the news that the Provincial Police would seek another adjournment (Taylor wrongly called it a "stay of proceedings") in Evans's section 98 preliminary hearing;
- a call by the Workers' Defense League for labour demonstra-

tions across the country, possibly including Princeton, on 16
December;
- ◆ the Coalmont miners' rejection of union organization;
- ◆ a further remand for Mike Kovich, the alleged stone-thrower; and
- ◆ another arrest of Patrick Driscoll "at the Princeton airport camp,
  where it is understood he was attempting to organize the relief
  workers"

With the Tulameen strike apparently settled, all that remained
of a contentious industrial nature was the continuing strike at
Wilson's Pleasant Valley mine, a subject to which Taylor returned
(when he was not inveighing against the Soviet takeover of
Princeton), arguing that a prolonged shutdown presented grave
economic risks to Princeton. "This property," he wrote,

> representing an investment of nearly $300,000 in plant and
> development, and recognized as one of the biggest potential indus-
> trial enterprises in the district, was giving seasonal employment
> to some fifty men. So far as can be learned, there were few or no
> complaints as to conditions there, but the union wished to make its
> schedule applicable to all collieries in the district. Acquainted with
> the situation, Mr. Wilson gave instructions that the mine was to be
> prepared for work as usual on the first day of the strike, Thursday,
> 1st December, and that if insufficient men turned up to carry on,
> the mine was to be closed. None was on hand, and the boilers were
> drained. The property was opened three years ago and has had a
> chequered career. It is understood that from a business standpoint
> it is a matter of indifference to the owners whether it is operated or
> not, though Mr. Wilson has always shown that he had the interest of
> the community at heart.[41]

The last sentence shows the contradiction running through
Taylor's thinking. He believed, or said he believed, that Wilson
operated the Pleasant Valley mine not for economic gain but for
the social benefits it creates, and when Wilson threatens to close
the mine he has "the interest of the community at heart." But
when the miners, who form the bulk of the community, go on

strike to advance their interests, they are threatening the economic prosperity of the town. But what was truly remarkable was the content of the over three thousand words devoted to "background," which clearly Taylor did not get through Wikipedia: the material came his way via some helpful soul in the Attorney-General's department, or perhaps a police contact. And what material!

The leader, "Is Local Agitation Inspired by Soviet? Workings of Labor League," was one thousand inspired words alleging Soviet interference in the affairs of Princeton. Its second paragraph describes the plot in broad strokes—

> in 1920 the Communist Party (the party) recognized the fact that the great mass of the workers failed to interest themselves in Communism or "red" revolution and the party decided that in order to make any practical headway, it would be necessary to break up the organizations which held the workers together namely, the trade unions.

—then Taylor goes on to give the good burghers of Princeton the "facts":

◆ The Trade Union Educational League (TUEL) was set up by the Red Labour Union to sow seeds of discord in the established trade unions.
◆ When unemployment became an issue, the Communist Party created another organization, the National Unemployed Workers' Association, to unite the employed and unemployed in a "United Front."
◆ After ten years of organizational work by the TUEL, the party felt strong enough to form its own labour central, and the Workers' Unity League was founded.
◆ Two other organizations were founded to help in the struggle: The Canadian Labour Defense League was formed to defend the working class; and the function of the Workers International Relief was "to arrange for the feeding and sheltering of

picketers during strikes and also to participate in hunger marches and demonstrations."

To show he was not alone in suspecting the Soviet Union of mischief in Canada, Taylor invoked the Ontario Court of Appeal—the previous year the court had heard the trial of Communist Party leader Tim Buck and others, and, in Taylor's characterization, found that

> The evidence proves that the Communist party of Canada is a member of the Communist International of Russia, and that instead of determining its own policies, purposes, teachings, and aims, it adopted and adopts those of the Communist International and therefore, that whatever are the policies, purposes and aims of the Communist International are also automatically those of the Communist party of Canada.[42]

If the Central Presidium of the Soviet Union was not daily focused on the destruction of Princeton's industry, then at least its purpose was the destruction of every such small town, not only in Canada but also in the industrialized west. This necessarily betokened a vast machinery of subversion, an army of spies and operatives, unlimited gold and preternatural intelligence. It was such a conspiracy as might justify the security activities of the RCMP and the B.C. Provincial Police, and the overzealous imagination of a small-town publisher such as Dave Taylor.

It should be noted, though, that Taylor was still cautious enough to temper his purpose with the appearance of even-handedness. In an editorial in the same issue, he asks:

> What is the status of the labor organizations which are establishing themselves in Princeton? No one can state with privilege that they are allied with the Soviet, however indirectly, and are thus illegal. However, there is sufficient indication of official views on the matter to justify at this vital time a close and careful scrutiny. If these are red organizations, this community is entitled to know it. If not, the quicker these allegations are denied the better. We print this week all

the evidence, real or circumstantial, we have been able to garner. If there is an equally strong alternative case we shall be just as glad to print it. This community should demand the truth.

OBSTRUCTING THE POLICE!!!

From the 16 August 1933 issue of *Unemployed Worker*.

If Princeton was indeed rife with Soviet apparatchiks, they would have been sharing the muddy streets with at least two of their counterparts from Victoria and Ottawa. The *Star* explained that "Mr. Adam Bell, deputy minister of labor for British Columbia, and Mr. F.E. Harrison, western representative of the federal department of labor, are in Princeton in connection with the local labor difficulties."

"We are not here," Mr. Harrison pointed out to the *Star*'s readers, "to settle the dispute on behalf of the employers, but in the interests of industrial peace." It was explained that their function was to investigate labor disputes, analyze the difficulties, suggest a solution, and act as intermediaries. They commented at length on the local situation, but most of their findings have already been well aired, while on other aspects they spoke reservedly. It was learned that they were none too well impressed with the form of organization embraced here.[43]

—this last presumably a crack at the union organization.

That same day, 15 December, Harrison made a preliminary report in which he gave a brief synopsis of the strike. He noted that the BC government was sufficiently concerned to send thirty constables, including ten mounted police; that the arrest of Evans had "created consternation in the ranks of the extremists"; that his place had been taken by Tom Bradley, who had been involved (as Evans himself had been) in the strike at Fraser Mills a year earlier; and that though "the cause of the present strike is due largely to communistic activities ... the management of the Tulameen Coal Mines is not without responsibility in the matter."

This surface even-handedness, so typical of the labour department of the federal government, was of course wrong: the strike was entirely provoked by the broken promise of the Tulameen owners; it was facilitated by the dynamic, focused and effective leadership of Arthur Evans, who, in what he brought to the fight, could just as easily have been a Conservative, a Liberal or a CCFer. As it was, the stupidity of the company, by its refusal to honour its promise "created a feeling of dissatisfaction which offered a fertile field for communistic activities."[44]

It appears no voice was raised to ask the relevance of all this, the connection between the return of a 10 percent wage reduction and the fortunes of the Communist International. We do not know whether other "well-informed men of reasonable views" wondered if Taylor and the other anti-Soviet zealots had not "slipped their treads" a trifle, but we do know that this was the start of a year-long invective-driven campaign in which Taylor imagined himself and other respectable citizens as being at war with the forces of international communism, and its avatar in Princeton, Arthur "Slim" Evans.

FOUR

TROUBLE IN THE LABOUR CAMPS

THE MINERS' STRUGGLE over pay cuts was not the only factor contributing to the atmosphere of class warfare that pervaded the town that winter. In late 1932, a federal relief camp opened just outside of Princeton.

One of the R.B. Bennett government's first responses to the depression was to establish a series of labour camps, first in B.C. and then in every province except Prince Edward Island. The relief camps put unemployed men to work building roads (including sections of the Trans-Canada highway), bridges, culverts, exhibition grounds, school grounds, mental hospitals, airports, military bases, and parks.

At first the pay consisted of food, accommodation, a clothing and toiletries allowance, medical and dental care, and two dollars a day. But the government of B.C., which housed over a third of all Canadian relief camp workers, considered this too costly a burden, and pressed Ottawa for lower standards in the camps. The federal government soon reduced the pay to $7.50 a month. When Bennett put the organization of the camps into the hands of Maj.-Gen. A.G.L. McNaughton and the Department of National Defence in May of 1933, the pay was further cut, to twenty cents a day, about $4.20 a month for a forty-four-hour work week.

Top: An idle moment in a 1930s relief camp bunkhouse, location unknown. Bottom: Inmates pose at Relief Camp No. 25 in March 1933. Cameras were strictly forbidden in the camps; the camp photos in this chapter were likely taken by the Department of National Defence.

The relief camps were intended for single, unemployed men, and replaced all other relief for such workers. The choice to move to the camps was nominally voluntary; nevertheless, they were organized along military principles. Camp inmates who disobeyed orders or regulations could face fines of up to one thousand dollars and three years' imprisonment. Camps were usually located away from towns to make the men disappear from urban life, where they were seen as a social danger. The camps were more or less explicitly designed not to provide work for the idle or even to undertake projects of public utility, but to inoculate against the "red menace": "By taking the men out of . . . the Cities . . . we were removing the active elements on which the 'Red' agitators could play," said McNaughton. "If we had not taken this preventative work, and did not continue . . . it was only a matter of time until we had to resort to arms to maintain order."[45]

Once these potential "Reds" were isolated far from urban centres, they were subjected to military-style regulations aimed at stifling dissent:

> The fatal error of the government was in placing the camps under the Department of National Defence and making the *King's Rules and Orders*—KR&O—the procedural Bible. This step guaranteed that whatever grievance did develop in the camps would be bottled up until it reached explosive proportions. No organization of any kind was permitted in any camp, and no petition could be circulated, and no committee could be formed to complain about anything. Anyone with a grievance could take it to the foreman of his gang, then appeal to the foreman of the sub-camp or the supervisor of the project. But he could do it only by himself without the vocal or moral support of a comrade. Anyone who tried to organize a protest in a camp faced expulsion and in some camps that meant being expelled in midwinter at the camp gates a hundred miles from the nearest habitation.[46]

Camps across the country were disheartening places to live, but the conditions in B.C.'s camps were widely regarded as the worst in the country.[47] A provincial government report noted that a great majority of the fifteen thousand inmates were physically unfit for work because they were undernourished and had been "living on the verge of starvation for some considerable time."[48] Although there was normally plenty of food, it was of the worst kind:

> The meat is always the cheapest beef, so tough that chewing is impossible, eggs are always storage eggs, milk is always dried, pickles such as beets which should be red may be as brown as oak, the same stewed fruit may appear at eight or nine consecutive meals, bread may be sour and coffee is known not by any aroma or flavour of its own, but by the difference between it and tea. [A camp inmate] can hardly forget for long there is no future . . . he is a failure, that in no sense whatever is he master of his destiny. Even his hours of rising and retiring are regulated, his comings and goings are marked and noted.[49]

The life was empty, and the work, meant to sustain the men's "work ethic," tended to have the opposite effect. For instance, because hard physical labour was exalted as a way of improving the character of the unemployed, relief camp labourers were often set to road work with picks and shovels while labour-saving bulldozers and rockblasting machines stood idle. The men saw no future ahead of them, just an indefinite stretch of pointless and ill-rewarded labour.

It was not long before they began to organize protest strikes and make demands. Some of these were for mundane matters such as better food, but others were for more far-reaching solutions. Although union organizers were ejected if discovered, organizers from the Workers Unity League worked the camps undercover, and found them to be fertile grounds.

★

Relief Camp No. 25 opened just north of Princeton in early December 1932. It housed 130 workers tasked with building an "intermediate landing field," one of a string of emergency landing fields the federal government was building across the coun-

try as it established air transportation infrastructure. Camp No.
25 was almost immediately the subject of complaints. According
to the *Star*,

> the story of the airport relief camp . . . has been one series of labor
> difficulties. The men have been gathered from many outside points,
> and the camp has also provided accommodation for a number of
> local men. The accommodation has been the general cause of the
> dissatisfaction, though disinterested men state that under the cir-
> cumstances, there seems to be little genuine ground for protest.
>
> They are employed in clearing an acreage for the airport site.
> The labor demand, it is said, is light. In return they are paid $6.00
> a month, boarded, bedded, and given various necessities, such as
> clothing, shaving material, etc.
>
> On one phase after another of the plan, they have from time
> to time risen in dissent, however. Officials up to this time have
> appeared to take a conciliatory view, aiming to keep the men in the
> camps, but they have evidently come to the point where they have
> decided to let the dissatisfied ones go their ways.
>
> There is a strong feeling that the dissatisfaction is not altogether
> one of genuine protest against camp conditions, but deliberately
> planned agitation.[50]

This "strong feeling," of course, did not come from the men
themselves but from those right-thinking members of the community, such as Taylor himself, to whom domestic discontent was
unthinkable: Any flames of discontent must have been fanned by
outside agitators. How could the men not be happy? Surely they
recognized that the story of the airport was

> the record of how waste land and idle men have been teamed to
> splendid advantage. In creating a national asset, another national
> asset—an army of single men thrown into the ranks of the unem-
> ployed—have been kept active and happy and have found in what
> may otherwise have been a depressing spell of impoverished inact-
> ivity, a new and interesting experience.[51]

Though there were other camps strung along the Hope–
Princeton highway, Camp No. 25 was close enough to town for

the relief camp workers to take more than a passing interest in the struggles of the local miners, and vice versa. The Workers' Unity League, and others of progressive views, fully understood the thinking behind the relief camps, and if the young unemployed were to be prevented from political action in the cities of Canada, then the WUL would take the politics to the workers in the camps.

Never was there a better locus for discussions on the nature of the world and what possibilities lay ahead for Canada: the men were far away from the cities, but also from the police forces and the daily defeatist propaganda, promulgated in every newspaper, claiming that the depression was a natural phenomenon about which nothing could be done.

The crisis of capitalism was the matter at hand: for the WUL, the struggles of union men, for a contract and their lost ten percent, and of the unemployed, for the opportunity to test the mettle of the government's depression policies, were but one fight. A golden opportunity presented itself, and the WUL took full advantage.

Not long after Slim Evans met his first group of Princeton miners, a trio of WUL organizers showed up in Princeton to prepare for Relief Camp No. 25. The most prominent of the three in the historical record is Patrick Driscoll (a.k.a James Lacey or Lacy, the leader of the picket line songs).[52] Driscoll was an active speaker and organizer, and would play a role in the upcoming events on behalf of both the unemployed workers and the miners. "Last month," reported the *Star* on 1 December, he "was a leader in the demonstration of dissatisfied unemployed who left the camps on the Hope–Princeton road." The two other WUL organizers sent to Princeton were Tom Bradley, who seems to have been the leader of the relief camp organizing effort, and who became a Canadian Labour Defence League organizer when that organization was established later in 1933 to represent relief camp workers; and Pete Lowe, sub-district organizer of the Young Communist League.[53]

Scenes from Relief Camp No. 25.

"Coupling their campaign," reported the *Star* on 1 December,

> with the efforts of local coalminers, the unemployed, after a long period of passive resistance, took action in condemning present arrangements for their care, and demanding a new basis with drastic changes. Following up a petition last week addressed to the provincial government asking for a guaranteed wage of eighty dollars a month for a five day week, seven hour day and other concessions, the unemployed on Wednesday, numbering over 300, marched to the government offices and presented a list of grievances to government agent L.A. Dodd.

Two other petitions were addressed to the government during the week: one making sweeping recommendations for a general revision of all economic relief efforts by the federal government; and another, which was also passed by the miners, demanding that the attorney-general remove from Princeton extra police reserves—described as "notorious strike-breakers and thugs, who have participated in strike-breaking at Timberlands, and Fraser Mills"—presumably sent to cope with the labour unrest.[54] The demands had been mostly generated elsewhere and adopted locally.[55] They represented not what might be achievable, but rather a declaration of basic principles: the conditions which every worker ought reasonably to expect in an ideal state which took seriously the notion that workers ought to be held harmless in an economic crisis they had not caused. The *Star* published them in full, presumably to demonstrate how out of touch workers were—but the demands must have raised the hearts of many a worker who was perhaps inclined to ask, "Well, why not?" As published in the *Star* of 1 December, they were:

- Non-contributory unemployment insurance, pending which is asked a cash allowance of $10 a week, and $2 for each dependent.
- Cash relief for all single men at the rate of $7 a week.
- No evictions of unemployed for debt; free light, rent, water, etc., at the expense of the provincial government.
- No discrimination on account of residence, nationality or sex.
- Representation for unemployed on all councils, etc., for relief, to

prevent discrimination and graft.
- Free schooling, supplies, and milk for children of unemployed.
- Cancellation of interest payments on Dominion and Provincial bonds.
- Cessation of all charity, military, police, and similar grants.
- No wages, no work. Wages to be 40 cents an hour for a seven-hour day and a five-day week; guaranteed twenty days' work a month, payment in cash, and free transportation to and from town to the minehead.
- Free hospital, medical, dental, etc. attention, without the humiliation or registration or questioning; free prescriptions, etc.
- No more deportations on the grounds of being public charges or for labour activities.[56]
- Repeal of Section 98 of the Criminal Code (vagrancy)[57] and sections 41 and 42 of the Immigration Act.
- Abolition of military camps and training for the unemployed.

As to existing camp conditions, in the absence of their abolition, the following were demanded:

- Supervision of all relief camps by a committee elected by the unemployed workers themselves.
- Three nourishing meals at cost, china dishes (instead of the tin plates the laborers were given to eat from), single spring beds, clean mattresses, and linen or flannelette sheets changed twice weekly.
- Clean towels, toilet soap, toilets cleaned daily; shower baths and radios in every bunkhouse, laundry and drying rooms.[58]
- First aid, medical supplies, and hospital treatment at government expense.
- Unrestricted mailing rights.
- Razor blades and haircutting equipment.
- No more camps to be built.
- An end to the ban on rod-riding, the technique for hitching rides on freight trains.
- A free clothing allowance for camp labourers, as follows: two shirts, two suits of underwear, one pair pants, one pair shoes, one pair gumboots, gloves, cap, hat, three pairs socks, and a mackinaw.
- An allowance of $15 a month.

The local issues had to do with the perceived ill treatment of specific individuals in Princeton—one worker was being hounded for not paying his son's hospital bill; a landlord attempted to evict six workers sharing a house for nonpayment of rent; a local foreman threatened to cut off relief workers who took part in political action; and the like. Dodd, Victoria's agent in Princeton, responded to each of these complaints, mostly by saying he had no authority to act.

On 15 December 1932, not a week after the camp opened, Driscoll was arrested by four Provincial Police officers for attempting to organize the relief workers, and charged under the ever-useful vagrancy section (238) of the Criminal Code. The *Unemployed Worker* (a publication of the WUL) reported the next week that "Comrade Driscoll was arrested for holding a meeting in a slave camp where the workers are sleeping on the floor, not being allowed to make bunks, working on an airport, 20¢ a day of 8 hours."[59] The next day twenty-seven men walked out over the issue.[60]

The *Star* on Christmas Eve reported in jocular fashion that "when twilight shadows lengthened, and the cold crept on, however, even the camp comforts they had despised began to look pretty good, and they trouped [sic] back to the camp. Foreman Lowe, on hearing their apologies, re-admitted the prodigals."

Originally Driscoll was charged not only under section 238 but also under section 98, but the second charge was stayed pending the outcome of Evans's section 98 trial.[61] Two other men were charged under the vagrancy section "after they had made themselves generally objectionable," according to the *Star*, and jailed 27 December for thirty days.

More trouble erupted in the new year. "A week of disturbances" over the food situation led to a visit to the camp by Colonel H.C. Grier, Divisional Supply Officer, who quickly quashed it. But the *Star* headline of 12 January 1933, "All Quiet at Airport Now," would prove to be premature.

On 25 January, between sixty and sixty-five men left the camp

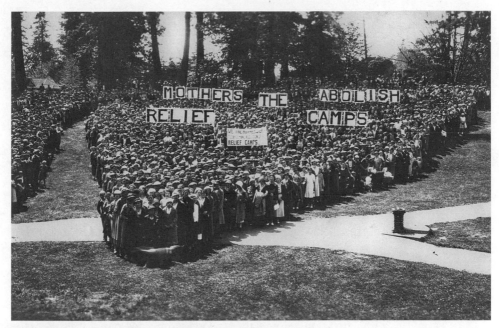

Mother's Day Committee members form a heart in Vancouver's Stanley Park on 12 May 1935 after leading a march of nearly fifteen hundred women and relief camp workers. The front banner reads "We the Mothers of Today Demand Abolition of the Relief Camps."

after a worker named Williams, a "ringleader," was discharged by the camp foreman for "general intractability and disobedience." The *Star* reported that they were paid up and told to leave: "Homeless and practically without funds, the men, many of whom are not residents of the district, were turned loose on the streets."[62] A week later, it reported that "most have been taken care of":

Sixteen have been admitted to the provincial relief camp at Copper Creek on the Hope–Princeton road. A number will get transportation this week to the Yellow Lake provincial relief camp, and a number have left town. The men caused no disturbance, though they have held meetings at the "Workers' Center" and have had conversations with local government officials. While remaining in town, the men have been taking the provincial government relief stipend of 25¢ per day, and some, at least, have slept at the "Workers' Center." At the provincial government relief camps the men will be on direct relief, receiving no monetary consideration of any kind, but being given board and lodging. It is not thought that they will prove a disturbing influence to the seventy men already quartered at this camp. In the summer it is understood, the men there will be put to work again on the construction of the Hope–Princeton road. For this they receive, in addition to accommodation, a small wage. The men who will go to the Yellow Lake camp on the Penticton road will go by truck from Princeton at the end of the week.[63]

The men were perhaps fortunate to escape. In March a writer calling himself "Fed-Up" reported to the *Unemployed Worker* that

there are about one hundred workers in this camp, mostly young from sixteen to twenty-five. Conditions here are terrible, workers being forced to work eight hours a day clearing land. The wage is only 20¢ a day. The shacks we live in consist of a wooden frame, with canvas pulled over them. Food is rationed out, a military issue of clothes is handed out. If men leave the camp the clothes are taken back by the Police. The K.K.K. come now and then, and burn a fiery cross to intimidate the workers. As Inspector MacDonald is a member of the K.K.K. we can see that the Govt. sanctions it, to make the workers put up with the rotten conditions.[64]

The coalminers' strike and the airport relief camp troubles were interwoven. It was a great advantage to the coal miners to have on hand 130 or so unemployed workers to augment meetings and marches, and for homeless and penniless miners to have access to a resource like the Workers' Center. But what held these two struggles together was the work of Evans and Driscoll and the WUL, to whom it was all one struggle. By persuading the camp workers that their unemployment was the fault "not of their stars" but of the system, they gave heart (and political direction) to men who would remember it throughout their lives.

FIVE

FIERY CROSSES & BEATINGS IN THE NIGHT

THE OPPOSITION TO the miners and their union had meanwhile taken on a menacing tone. Local citizens and the Provincial Police began a campaign of intimidation through harassment, threats, and actual force. It began with a powerful visual symbol.

The week after the Tulameen strike was declared won, with the return of the 10 percent pay cut and the recognition of the union, opposition forces took a curious step to demonstrate that they were not beaten: on Sunday, 18 December 1932, a burning cross appeared on a hillside overlooking the town.

Under the banner "Fiery Cross Makes Its Appearance Here," the *Star* reported it the following Thursday, in light-hearted form:

> Visions of white clad figures and midnight visitations flitted before the eyes of the good and law-abiding people of Princeton on the Sabbath as the spectre of the fiery cross loomed on the hillside, the symbol of the Ku Kux Klan, the flame that can only be quenched in blood. There it flared, unmistakeably, about 7 p.m., in fact some folks report that there was one on either side of the town.
>
> Two provincial police officers went to investigate but found nothing but the glowing embers.
>
> Genuine or no, the origin of the event is as deep a mystery as any genuine Ku Kux [sic] warning ever was. There are all sorts of

guesses as to its significance, but no one including the police seems to take a very serious view of the matter. Perley says perhaps it was a move to make people do their confessing more regularly about the Christmas time. The devil says he still sleeps with his door open but has moved his [word illegible] closer. The customary three days at any rate, passed without incident. There were some rumours about shots being heard but police believe that the "shots" were backfires of a balky carburetor.[65]

It is hardly surprising, given Taylor's disingenuousness concerning this "deep ... mystery," that he did not report, as the *Unemployed Worker* did, the message left at the site:

TAKE NOTICE
THE FIERY CROSS HAS SPOKEN
AGITATORS TAKE WARNING AND MOVE
OR SUFFER THE CONSEQUENCES
THE KLAN

The *Worker* also reported protests against the "present terrorism of police and gangsters," including marches of the strikers and the unemployed, and a petition signed by "twenty four businessmen" and several fraternal lodges "demanding the withdrawal of the hooligans."[66]

Ku Klux Klan cross burnings may seem an oddity in British Columbia in the early thirties; the original Klan formed during the Reconstruction period in the United States (1865–1877) to fight the newly established freedom of southern black people. But it was revived in the 1920s and 1930s, and widened its targets to include Jewish people, Catholics, labour activists, and communists.[67]

Six months before its appearance in Princeton the Klan had emerged in the Crowsnest Pass to oppose strikes taking place in the coalfields—on the night of 13 May 1932 a giant fiery cross appeared on Goat Mountain, visible to the citizens of Blairmore down in the valley. The Klan had come to the prairies in the late-1920s and the Crowsnest Pass, given the large number of Eastern European miners in the area, was selected as an anti-immigration, anti-union, and anti-communist battleground. An RCMP report of 6 November 1932 titled "Activities of the Ku Klux Klan in the Crowsnest Pass: Secret" noted that the Klan "had over one hundred [members] on the roster in the Pass, all of whom are good citizens from between the towns of Pincher Creek and Natal."[68] As in Princeton, threatening notices reading "Reds Beware—Watch Your Step—KKK" had been pinned to the doors of union houses and on the union hall. The same pattern of intimidation seen in the Pass—a Citizens' League ostensibly neutral but in reality opposing the strikers; attacks and arrests on picket lines; the continual police searches of unionists' houses offices; and attempts by mine owners to organize scabbing—had come to Princeton.[69]

A dozen local men established the Princeton branch of the Klan on the very eve of the miners' strike, 30 November 1932. An affidavit by D.E. Wibber from 5 May the following year swore that, on that evening,

> Claud [sic] Snowden approached me to attend a meeting at Gregory's office which I did. The meeting being held for the purpose of organizing the Ku Klux Klan. Upon my arrival there I was told to stand on one side while they discussed my recruiting. Those present were: Claud Snowden, Gregory, J. Hughey, F. Parks, Prideux, Ted and Elmer Burr and Ed Burr, Senior, Chas. Watson, F. Chisler, Art Turner and Leatherby.[70] For certain reasons (the reason I found out latter [sic] to be, was that some of them were doubtful as to my reliability, stating that I could be easily swayed for a bottle of rum): I was tilled [sic] that I was not needed. Don Thompson asked me if I lined up [for] the K.K.K. I told him of my being rejected and he said, "Don't have anything to do with the K.K.K. because they were taking the law into their own hands and by so doing, were breaking the law."

One of the Klan's slogans, "One Flag, One School, One Language," offers clues to its appeal among certain segments of the population. "One Flag" referred to the British Red Ensign: Canada was British, the thinking went, and foreigners arriving in Canada should not bring their old national disputes. "One Language" spoke to the same notion, with the added element of opposition to Quebeckers. "One School" was an argument for a cultural melting pot rather than a mosaic, which appealed to Ontario Orangemen and their objection to Roman Catholic schools.

✲

Trouble had again erupted at the Tulameen mine over Christmas. The miners stopped work on Boxing Day after four men, John D'Angelo, John Dandrea, Martin Berkich, and H.F. Hayes, were fired for refusing to work on Christmas Eve (the traditional day of celebration for Eastern Europeans).

This had been brewing since the miners learned that the mine would be operating on Christmas Eve and they would be expected to show up for work that evening as usual. The men held a meeting, decided they would not work that day, and informed Superintendent Bennett. He told them that any man who did not show up for work on Christmas Eve would be fired; the four men did not show up, and were fired.

After another meeting, the men decided to walk out in support of their fired comrades. Over the next week, following another visit by the directors, John Bennett resigned as superintendent,[71] all the scabs who had been hired in the interim were fired, and the four fired men were rehired. The firebosses who had been prosecuted for "failing to maintain a position of trust" were also rehired, and the prosecution of ten strikers, which had been initiated by Bennett and District Mines Inspector J.G. Biggs under the Industrial Disputes Act, was abandoned. The Tulameen miners returned to work on Tuesday, 3 January 1933, having achieved all their main objectives in the walk-out.

Judging by the violence that followed, this unequivocal victory for the union must have incensed the town's establishment and the local Klan members. During the previous month they had been harassing John Beronich, a local miner who was active in the union; he would later swear in an affidavit that "on many occasions, papers and magazines which I was Agent for . . . were confiscated by the British Columbia Police Force" and that "during my residence in . . . Princeton my home was searched both night and day and in many cases amounting to three or four times the same day and was also searched three and four times per day either on the street or in the Police Station." He also said that between 6 December 1932 and 13 January 1933 he had received two letters "at different times which read as follows: 'The Klan will take you for a ride' and signed as follows: 'K.K.K.'"[72]

On the evening of Friday, 13 January 1933, just before midnight, Beronich was returning from the bowling alley to his home on Allison Flats. As he crossed the the Tulameen River on the Brown Bridge, where Bridge Street ends in a junction with the road to Tulameen and Coalmont, he noticed two cars parked on either side of the bridge. As he crossed, the cars blocked both sides of the bridge, trapping him in the middle. Two groups of men emerged and asked if he was John Beronich. All but one of them were masked and, according to a report in the *Unemployed Worker*, wearing "big white hoods."[73] When Beronich refused to answer they attacked. It appears to have been a brief affray; after beating him they attempted to get him into one of the cars, but he resisted, and bit the hand of one of his assailants. Beronich was found by another man and brought to the Tulameen Hotel, where the police and the doctor were summoned. They both thought he was drunk, though evidence in the subsequent court case indicated there were lumps on each side of his head and his mouth was filled with blood.

After interviewing Beronich the police arrested and charged with assault the one attacker Beronich was able to identify. A hearing was set for 23 January 1933. The night before the trial another burning cross appeared above town, and Taylor again romanticized it in the *Star*:

The "fiery cross", symbol at once of terrorism and stern, unrelenting justice again made its appearance on the hills of Princeton Sunday night, just before the trial of a local man accused of being a member of the organization supposed to be responsible for its presence.[74]

Beronich testified that the one man he was able to recognize was Teddy Burr, a mechanic, son of the local garage owner, and, along with his brother and father, member of the local Ku Klux Klan. Police testified that they had interviewed Burr at his house within the hour. He was wearing pants over his pyjamas, but seemed sleepy, and denied that he had left the house after he returned from the garage at half past ten. Both the Burr family's cars were outside the house and neither showed evidence of being driven—both radiators were cold. The charge against Burr was dismissed.[75]

Teddy Burr appeared in the papers again the next month, this time in connection with some counter-propaganda at the airport relief camp. In two February *Unemployed Worker* articles, a writer identifying himself as "P.D." (Patrick Driscoll, perhaps) warns the *Worker*'s readership of the anti-union activities of the KKK and the Canadian Legion (the only mentions of the Legion's role in the Princeton labour troubles). In one article "P.D." names a Canadian Legion operative:

> Last week a very notorious man, who could not do a days work if he tried, has been engaged by the bosses to get up a position in Princeton with scab labour. This man "Windy Bill" is a veteran soldier, who fought for his country (HIS COUNTRY) and now the wonderful hero is fighting for the state in their drive to starve the men, women and children to submission and has all the police protection he wants.

In the other, headlined "CLASS JUSTICE AT PRINCETON," "P.D." denounces the efforts of Teddy Burr. "Comrades," he writes,

I want to call your attention to the treacherous role that the Canadian Legion is playing in Princeton in calling on the youth of this town and of the Air Port Camp to act as strike breakers.

By putting on concerts in this camp, giving speeches to fire their patriotism, calling on them to come down and clean up on the workers who are nothing but a bunch of "foreigners and Reds", lolling them to sleep and taking their minds off their own grievances — starvation conditions under which they themselves are living; giving them songs such as this [a song was enclosed] to make them forget their troubles many of these young workers are now scabbing due to the Canadian Legion and the K.K.K. led by a dirty, lousy, fascist, strike breaking individual by the name of Ted Burr, son of a local Tsar, a conservative political heeler.[76]

A settlement at Pleasant Valley had begun to take shape shortly after Christmas 1932, and soon bore results. It was put together by J.G. Biggs, the district mines inspector; Adam Bell, the deputy labour minister in B.C.; and F.E. Harrison, the western representative of the federal labour department. The sticking point throughout was the question of union recognition, though Wilson had said he would recognize a pit committee. Biggs tried on several occasions to meet with the men rather than with the union leadership, but on each occasion the union called a meeting at the same time, and so the men had not presented themselves to Biggs. The terms of the would-be settlement were outlined in the *Star* of 29 December:

- A general wage increase definitely set forth in a Schedule, publication of which is not permitted. Miners were to get $4.60 a day.
- Contract rates to be on the same basis as when worked stopped.
- The company will recognize a pit committee appointed from and by the employees.
- The company declines to recognize the Mine Workers' Union of Canada.

A public meeting was arranged for Monday, 6 February, two weeks after the charge against Burr was dropped. The board of

Likely the Princeton Board of Trade elected in 1932. Back row, left to right: 1–3 and 6, unknown; 4, W.A. Wagenhauser, proprietor of the Princeton Department Stores; 5, Edgar E. Burr, owner of Burr Motors. Front row: George G.M. Harmon, manager of the Bank of Commerce and vice president of the board; Dave Taylor, secretary; Percy W. Gregory, president; unknown.[77]

trade, anxious to get out in front of the parade, held its own meeting immediately prior, and some thirty-eight members "decided that the time had come when they must take a stand against further activities against so-called 'Red' organizations in Princeton."

"Who is running this town?" asked one citizen, as he explained how the present agitation had crippled the business life of the community, and pointed out that property interest had suffered heavily, and with continued unreasoned agitation the future of the town would be ruined. He pointed out that the trouble was caused by men's minds being poisoned by paid agitators, who had not a cent's worth of interest in the community. "They call these men who work 'scabs'," he said. "There is no trouble at the Pleasant Valley mine, and yet families are being deprived of their livelihood. The men who take this view are scabs against their own families."

The meeting then adjourned so the board members could attend the public meeting, at which about one hundred were in attendance. The terms above, particularly the day rate of $4.60, had persuaded many of the men that they could put off the question of unionization. "Circumstances leading up to the meeting were explained," reported the *Star*, "and the terms of the contract read. Candidates for employment then voted to accept the terms, and forty signed to go to work. Mr. P.W. Gregory, President of the Princeton Board of Trade, conveyed to the men the information that the business men had endorsed their move."

They more than endorsed the move: a dozen of them formed a guard of honour, as it were, for the first miners to resume work on the bitterly cold morning (−32°F) of 9 February. Perhaps they were expecting an active picket, but they found none.

That day's *Star* reported that the dam had broken

when forty or more men approached the management and intimated that they were weary of the tie-up, willing to do honest work under honest working conditions, and quite unconcerned with any outside or local influence that has developed and seeks to stop them. Assured that they had moral support of a responsible representation of the citizens, they registered for work under the terms of a new agreement, to which they would automatically subscribe as they take employment.

The Union bowed to the inevitable and on 12 February called off the strike.

Labour peace had now been restored to the whole district—both the Tulameen and Pleasant Valley mines were back at work, with increased pay for all, and Evans was facing charges that carried a maximum sentence of twenty years' imprisonment. In a banner headline on 16 February 1933, the *Star* declared "Industrial Peace Here Once Again."

SIX

UNLAWFUL ASSOCIATIONS

BEFORE RECOUNTING THE events of spring 1933, it is worth telling the story of how section 98, under which Evans was charged, came into existence and was finally removed from the Criminal Code. It first saw light in September 1918 under the War Measures Act; as the First World War was coming to a close, authorities were concerned about the return of the veterans from Europe and the enthusiasm many Canadian workers showed for the Russian revolution. C.H. Cahan, a Montreal lawyer, was instructed to make recommendations "in respect to the existing regulations for safeguarding the public interests [sic] against enemy aliens."[78] Cahan noted in his report that

> the Russians, Ukrainians and Finns who are employed in the mines, factories and other industries in Canada are now being saturated with the socialistic doctrines which have been proclaimed by the Bolsheviki faction in Russia. . . . I have before me a mass of literature, filled with most pernicious and seditious teaching, which is even now, in large quantities, being secretly circulated in Canada. . . . Since the outbreak of the present war, revolutionary groups of Russians, Ukrainians and Finns have been organized throughout Canada, and are known as the Social Democratic Party of Canada, the Ukrainian Revolutionary Group, the Russian Revolutionary Group, and others.

Less than two weeks after Cahan submitted his report, Robert Borden's government introduced order-in-council P.C. 1918-2384, which banned fourteen organizations. In language drawn from American statutes,[79] it "'deemed unlawful,' — 'while Canada is engaged in war' — any association whose purpose"

> is to bring about any governmental, political, social, industrial, or economic change within Canada by the use of force, violence, or physical injury to person or property, or by threats of such injury, or which teaches, advocates, advises or defends the use of force, violence, or physical injury to person or property or threats of such injury in order to accomplish such change or for any other purpose, or which shall by any means prosecute or pursue such purpose.[80]

It was also an offence, punishable by one-to-five years' imprisonment, to belong to or wear the badge of such an organization, or to "sell, speak, write or publish anything" as a representative of such organizations. Any property belonging to such an organization was seizable by the state. Anyone who knowingly permitted a meeting of such an organization in premises he or she owned or rented could be fined five thousand dollars and jailed for up to five years. Once the Crown had proven that an accused had attended meetings, spoken in support, or distributed literature of such an organization, the accused bore a reverse onus to prove that they were not a member. Finally, meetings conducted in Russian, Finnish, Ukrainian, or the languages of any country with which Canada was at war, "except church meetings or meetings for religious services only," were outlawed. This was a declaration of open season on all kinds of leftist organizations, and within weeks, dozens of people had been fined and jailed.

As it was a wartime order-in-council, P.C. 1918-2384 was repealed 1 April 1919. But the government was already thinking about a permanent replacement for it, and a month later set up a House of Commons committee to propose amendments to the Criminal Code in the area of sedition. The committee tabled its report 6 June 1919, in the middle of the Winnipeg General

Strike. It recommended an amendment to the code along the lines of P.C. 1918-2384. With little debate in the House, and even less in the Senate, the bill to amend the code was carried, and section 98 became law. Whereas P.C. 1918-2384 carried a maximum prison sentence of five years, section 98 raised it to twenty years, and added a new clause, subsection 6, allowing for search and seizure:

> (6) If any judge of any superior or county court, police or stipendiary magistrate, or any justice of the peace is satisfied by information on oath that there is reasonable ground for suspecting that any contravention of this section has been or is about to be committed he may issue a search warrant under his hand, authorizing any peace officer, police officer, or constable with such assistance as he may require, to enter at any time any premises or place mentioned in the warrant, and to search such premises or place and every person found therein and to seize and carry away any books, periodicals, pamphlets, pictures, papers, circulars, cards, letters, writings, prints, handbills, posters, publications or documents which are found on or in such premises or place or in the possession of any person therein at the time of such search and the same, when seized may be carried away and may be forfeited to His Majesty.[81]

This useful clause allowed, as we have seen, endless and repeated searches, at all hours of the day and night, of union halls and organizers' and workers' homes. It also allowed the police to seize in-transit literature sent to Princeton—the Princeton organizers frequently complained that bundles of newspapers were broken open and seized.

Section 98 was not used until nearly a decade after its introduction, partly because of the tendency of oppressive laws such as this to backfire. The section was not used against the Winnipeg strikers—other laws, such as unlawful assembly and sedition, were used instead, and those convicted soon became popular heroes. In the 1920 provincial election Manitobans elected eleven out of fifty-five labour-affiliated candidates, three of whom were in prison for their actions in the general strike, and the next year sent two strike leaders, A.A. Heaps and J.S. Woodsworth, to the House of Commons.

The 1920s was a time of growth for the whole of the labour movement and its various affiliated parties. The trade unions were the first groups to oppose section 98; even the respectable Trades and Labour Congress unions recognized the threat implicit in the legislation. During the December 1919 trial of R.B. Russell, one of those charged following the Winnipeg General Strike, Judge Metcalfe's address to the jury made that threat clear — the sympathy strike was a tool of the trade for the union movement, yet Judge Metcalfe thought it reeked of violence:

> Mr. Russell gave us his idea of a sympathetic strike. He said, "When a dispute originates between an employer and his employees, and when the labour organizations see that organization being beat, they come to their assistance by calling a strike to force their employers to bring force to bear upon the original disputants to make settlement." That is Russell's definition given in the box. . . . Force, force, force. . . .
>
> To walk around about, for instance, to a place where people are employed in large numbers, and to "boo," gentlemen of the jury, as much terror may be inspired through that as by two or three fighting chaps coming along with bludgeons. Take it from me, in strikes you can incite terror without hitting a man over the head. You can incite terror of starvation; you can incite terror of thirst. Is not that quite as effective as inciting by bodily violence? . . . If it is possible that picketing can be done in this country, then the lawful method of picketing is so ineffective that it is a reasonable inference that in strikes of this class, unlawful means would be intended to be applied.[82]

J.S. Woodsworth took up the case against section 98 as soon as he was elected to the House of Commons in 1921. He moved a motion for its abolition annually from that year on, and in 1925 made its abolition one of three conditions for continued support of the minority Liberal government of Mackenzie King.

Following the successful election of a majority Liberal government, the Commons moved for repeal in 1926, but the Senate, still dominated by the Conservative Party, voted it down. This occurred every year from 1926 to 1930. This was true also of a parallel move to amend the Immigration Act to prevent the deportation without trial of "aliens." This, as we have seen, spoke to an element of the Princeton strikes—the notion that peace-loving Princeton was being overrun with Eastern European "aliens" who neither belonged nor should belong there, despite the fact that they formed a large minority in the town.

The first prosecution under section 98 failed. In 1929 four young women, all supporters of the Communist Party, were charged with distributing leaflets "advocating force, violence and terrorism to effect governmental, industrial or economic change,"[83] and all were acquitted, as was the indicted printer of the leaflets.

The government was better prepared for the next trial. They hoped to have the Communist Party itself declared an illegal organization, in which case simple charges of membership could be brought against any individual member, without having to prove each time that the party advocated the use of violence. In 1931 the party offices in Toronto were raided and eight leaders of the party were charged and tried before a jury: Tim Buck, Tom Ewen (McEwen), Malcolm Bruce, Tom Hill, John Boychuk, Sam Carr, Matthew Popovich and Tom Cacic. The presiding judge was William H. Wright, "a pillar of the United Church" who had recently sentenced Aarvo Vaara, a communist newspaper editor, to six months in jail for insulting King George V.[84]

The prosecution built its case on the connection between the Canadian Communist Party and the Comintern. This was not difficult, as the Canadian party described itself as "a section of the Communist International." Much of the evidence was derived from Soviet documents, but, as Frank Scott reported in *Queen's Quarterly*,

> there was no evidence of any reliable sort to show that the party had ever committed any overt act of violence within Canada. . . . The accused were tried, not for past or present violence, but for member-

ship in an organization that, it was contended, aimed at and advocated the use of violence to effect changes in Canada some time
in the future. . . . It was Russian documents rather than Canadian
which constituted the bulk of the evidence dealing with revolution.[85]

Nonetheless, the prosecution succeeded, and the eight leaders
were sentenced to prison terms varying between three and five
years.

The appeal was heard in January 1932 before Chief Justice
William Mulock, who only months before had "called publicly
for stamping out the 'treasonable communist virus' that would
'destroy the sacredness of marriage, nationalize women, extin-
guish the love of parents for their children, and abolish home
life.'" The appeal court threw out one count of the indictment,
"seditious conspiracy," but upheld the convictions "for being
members and officers of an unlawful association."[86]

Police and prosecutors recognized that section 98 convictions
would be hard to come by, but this "unlawful association" clause
promised encouraging results. Subsection 5 stated that

> any owner, lessee, agent or superintendent of any building, room,
> premises or place who knowingly permits therein any meeting of
> an unlawful association or any subsidiary association or branch or
> committee thereof, or any assemblage of persons who teach, advo-
> cate, advise or defend the use without authority of the law, of force,
> violence or physical injury to person or property, or threats of such
> injury, shall be guilty of an offence under this section and shall be
> liable to a fine of not more than five thousand dollars or to imprison-
> ment for not more than five years, or to both fine and imprisonment.

In B.C., government counsel W.H. Bullock-Webster, who would
later prosecute Evans under section 98, thought the unlawful
association subsection might be useful in harassing unions, the
Communist Party, or any other relevant organization. "I admit
that this procedure would be bluff," he noted in September 1932
to the RCMP Commissioner, "but I think it can be so strongly
presented that the effect would be satisfactory."[87] Satisfactory, that

is, to the authorities, who believed that no type of political activity when carried out by Communists was proper or legitimate.

Bluff it may well have been, but it was used in Princeton in April 1933 to kick the union out of its hall, to prevent it from meeting anywhere indoors in the Princeton area, and to stop Evans from speaking in halls in Princeton and Tulameen (and eventually throughout the riding he contested in that fall's provincial election).[88]

Though the government had met with some success in its use of section 98, it used it sparingly; after Buck et al., the next person charged was Arthur Evans, whose trial is the subject of chapter nine. Very few prosecutions proceeded, though there were a few, and a few convictions. Evans was charged again in Regina in 1935, but the charges were dropped before the case went to trial.[89] Why the cold feet? Section 98 scholar Richard Fidler argues that a memorandum from Joseph Sedgwick, a noted Canadian criminal law expert, to the

Slim Evans on the March 1936 cover of *Unity*.

Ontario attorney general may well have expressed the settled view of the government: "One effect of the Communist trial has been to make martyrs of the eight who were convicted, and their incarceration has furnished a rallying point for the forces of unrest."[90]

Nevertheless, the struggle to remove section 98 continued, led by the Canadian Labor Defense League (CLDL). They brought a petition to the House of Commons with 66,617 signatures in favour of the repeal of the section (and of sections of the Immigration Act regarding deportations). On the same day, 22 February 1932, J.S. Woodsworth (who would found and lead the CCF later that year) moved the repeal in the House.

The tone of the Tory times are caught in Minister of Justice Hugh Guthrie's response the following year to Woodsworth's next attempt to repeal section 98. Responding to the receipt of letters and petitions from the CLDL, Guthrie said,

> I learn of the activities of this association through petitions from every quarter of this dominion. I am not overstating the case when I say that I have hundreds and hundreds of them. I have now ceased to acknowledge receipt of them. I merely hand them over to the mounted police in order that a record may be kept of the names and addresses of the people who sign them, and I make this statement so that the petitioners may know what I do with them. . . . I can assure the house that in long petitions there does not appear a single Anglo-Saxon or French-Canadian name—nothing but names of foreigners, unpronounceable names for the most part.[91]

It would clearly require the election of a new government to see any alteration to the law. That election came 14 October 1935, when a Liberal landslide swept away the Bennett government: 173 Liberals to 39 Conservatives. Such was the antipathy towards Conservatism that they would not regain power until Diefenbaker's election twenty-three years later. The Liberals were committed to the repeal, which finally came 19 June 1936.

SEVEN

The Spring of Discontent

THE RESUMPTION OF work at Pleasant Valley in February 1933 may well have occasioned industrial peace, but there was no sign of political peace. The attack on Evans and his supporters continued with the closing of the Workers' Center. On 6 April, under the headline "Communist Hall Will Be Closed: Police Serve Notice to Owner Under Section 98," Taylor reported:

> The Workers' Center, headquarters for the past six months of various organizations affiliated to the Canadian Labor Defense League, said to have their inspiration in Moscow, has been ordered closed as from 23rd April.
>
> Notice has been served on W.H. Thomas, owner of the building, that if he allows further use of the premises by these organizations he is liable to prosecution under provisions of the criminal code of Canada. Mr. Thomas has in turn instructed the occupants to vacate the premises by the date specified.

Taylor was ecstatic: his accompanying editorial crowed over the decision. "The latest edict," he wrote,

> will have one splendid effect, we hope. It will bring these meetings into the open air, where the unsympathetic among the audience cannot be excluded and the key turned at the opposite moment. There is of course another alternative. It may drive the followers into private houses. There is a good deal of misconception about what one

can do in the sanctity of one's own home. For instance, if you make home brew it is quite all right to drink it yourself and to give it to the rest of your family; but should your neighbor come in, that is a very different matter. Yes, knowing the intricacies of the law is quite a science. For every one time most of us fall foul of it, there are ninety-nine when we have previously done so without detection and like as not without realization. But at times like this it pays to be careful.

Taylor went further still: not only did section 98 apply to public halls, but also private houses:

> In no case is this delusion more unfortunate than under section 98. What applies to the Workers' Center applies equally to your own home or to your room even, and if you are the owner you are equally culpable whether you are a member of the organization, or whether you are present or not. It is only fair that people should know this—but unfortunately the law is not very much concerned about whether you know it or not.[92]

Taylor had previously targeted primarily Evans, and through him the Communist Party and the new union. Here he goes further. He threatens every miner and every person who ever heard Evans speak. With the strike over and the town back to normal, as it were, why did Taylor not let the matter drop?

The "industrial peace" in Princeton lasted almost two months. On 7 April the Tulameen mine company dropped the bombshell news that they would again impose the "seasonal reduction in wages of 10%" of the previous year. The wage cut would commence 1 May 1933, and if the workers did not agree to it the mine would be closed. This was, of course, a violation of the agreement that the union had made with the company. This is how the *Star* reported the facts:

> Princeton is faced with the loss of its principal and almost sole pay roll unless the Mine Workers' Union will permit its employees to accept a ten per cent reduction at the Tulameen Coal Mine.
> Manager T.M. Wilson has announced that the wage cut will be

effective 1st May, and that failing a response to this appeal the mine will be closed indefinitely.[93]

Of course, the Mine Workers' Union consisted of working Princeton miners, and could not "permit its employees" to do anything because the miners were not its employees — the union, having a democratic structure, could do only what its members chose to do.

Nevertheless, Taylor went on to assert that the union's principal members were not coal miners themselves, the union was not democratically controlled, and if a free and secret vote were held the men would accept the cut. In Taylor's view, if the union did not immediately accede to the peremptory demand of the mine, it would be solely responsible for the loss of Princeton's payroll. Such was Taylor's "neutrality."

The news of the demanded cut and the confrontation that it surely heralded seem to have sent Taylor into a paroxysm of anger. The paper ran several pieces in a variety of forms, all attacking Slim Evans, who became the public face of the miners. On 20 April the following poem and an inscription from a mock tombstone[94] (pictured on the facing page) appeared on the front page of the *Star*:

> Tread lightly, Pilgrim, on this sterile ground;
> 'Twas once a thriving, bustling town.
> When the Reds came and took it o'er,
> Prosperity went to a kindlier shore.
> Evanskovich and his cohorts rule;
> The "Red Flag" is now sung in school.
> The mines are closed, the town is dead,
> The children now cry out for bread.
> So, Pilgrim, walk with muted tread;
> You are passing o'er dishonoured dead.
> Through cowardice, we must allow
> That Evanskovich is ruling now.

Inside is a letter by a "Hillcrest and Drumheller" that criticizes Evans for travelling "first class" and seeking a "sympathy vote" by

George Shorthouse (left) and Claude Snowden pose with a piece of agitprop.

parading his wife and child around, and claims he is only interested in cheating money from the working class. The issue also contains a letter purporting to be from a Communist agent in Moscow to a British Communist Party member (perhaps akin to the famous "Zinoviev letter"[95]) that, according to Taylor, "fell into the hands of the British police, [and] reveals the machinations of the Soviet Union, manifestation of which has been gravely felt in the Princeton district." The letter is enjoyable enough to reproduce in full:

EKKI.147.PV 1RE March 1933

We have your request for funds. 1000£ will be forwarded in the usual way. It is necessary at this juncture to sound the temper of the English proletariat. To this end a closely centralized organization must be formed to take the place of the present cells. The cells must continue their work in the same way as in the past, but it is imperative that their leaders get in touch with us with greater ease than is possible now. We suggest that the present quarters at either RK or T be used as headquarters. The cells must use every means possible to cause unrest in the Army, Navy and Air Force.

The Police Force, as a body cannot be approached, but there are members who would undoubtedly work for us if enough money was paid to them. We leave it in your hands to find these men and to sound them. We are satisfied with the way you are undermining the trade unions. You must impress upon the individual members of these bodies that their leaders are only a part of the Capitalistic system, and that it would be to their advantage to break away from them until it is possible to form a branch of the Profintern in England. We think you have gone as far as possible in taking over the leadership of the unemployed. You must exploit them to form a shield for your other activities. The time is not yet ripe for a general revolution in England, therefore we leave the arranging of details for May 1 in your hands. No useful purpose could be served by the orders being issued by us, and there is a great danger of written plans going astray (certain information has been published by one of your Sunday papers anent our plans for May).

We agree that Mass demonstrations on May 1 will be of help in sounding the feelings of the people, and of ascertaining the leanings of the people of England towards the Cause. Speakers and members of cells must endeavor to cause minor rioting on that day to see how far the support of the general population can be relied upon. We support you in this but do not think that any rioting on a large scale should take place on that day as in our previous instructions we adhere to May 1936 as being the most probable date for a general outbreak.

With reference to the three new agents, these must be put under observation for a time before any decision is arrived at. Ascertain full details as to their associates and friends to eliminate any possibility of their being Police or Press agents.

Your propaganda work must still be done in secret, the small Guilds and Societies you have formed must continue to cloak the presence of known revolutionaries, but you cannot come out into the open until we are of certain numerical strength.

We appreciate your anxiety about working in the dark, but would point out that until sufficient reliable leaders have been found, and we have obtained a greater numerical strength than we have at present, you are liable to undo all the good you have done and are doing by admitting into the Executive supposed adherents to the Third International who are nothing more than Reformers and "Center" elements. There is also the possibility of the Press obtaining information in this way, which must be avoided if possible.

Further instructions will be issued next month. A copy of this has been forwarded to our agents in Liverpool, Dublin and Newcastle. Will you forward copies to Manchester, Bristol and Cardiff.[96]

The *ad hominem* attacks on Evans continued the following week. Two letters were published, one from "Anti Red" noting that some eighty "foreigners" are to be deported (or should be; the exact meaning is unclear); the other from "Tommy Atkins" (slang for a British soldier in World War I) suggesting that "we are ready once more to go over the top. We are only waiting for the word of command."[97]

Another letter, from "A Princeton Citizen and Worker," reports that "my wife was handed a typewritten notice two days ago with the heading 'So this is Canada.' This notice refers to Blind Bill Nicholson, and I happen to know some of the facts

of the case." Though we have not found a copy of this notice, the *Unemployed Worker* of 4 February reports that it claimed that "Blind Bill" Nicholson, a pro-union ex-miner, was to be turned out of his house. Nicholson had been blinded in a mining accident in 1906 and was on a disability pension, but he was a strong union supporter, always ready to put up any union man needing a bed for the night. The writer noted that the owner of Nicholson's cabin had told Nicholson that "he may want the cabin for himself shortly." Far from being unfair to Nicholson, the writer claimed, a better home was waiting for him: "Some time ago the government arranged for all blind persons to be comfortably housed in a home especially provided for that purpose, at the coast,

"Blind Bill" Nicholson led a hunger march protest in Victoria on 4 April 1933.

where they could get proper care and treatment, in clean and suitable pleasant surroundings, instead of the filth and dirt that blind people who cannot do things for themselves are likely to live in." The *Unemployed Worker* reported Nicholson as saying he'd rather go to Oakalla, the provincial jail.

The last letter worth mentioning was by John Cherkosh on behalf of the union; it expresses their outraged reaction to the contents of the previous week's paper. and denounces the claims as baseless propaganda. Taylor appended to this letter his own remarks, which counter every one of Cherkosh's claims and advance in full the company's claim that it could not pay the full rate. Taylor prefaced his rebuttal by claiming, with outrageous gall, that "It has always been our policy to serve all interests in this community."

✳

In response to the mine's most recent 10 percent pay cut proposal the board of trade redoubled its efforts to break what it considered the union's hold on the miners. It sent telegrams to the minister of mines and labour, who happened to be the local MLA, W.A. McKenzie, urging him to come to Princeton to assist personally in the crisis.[98] No response was forthcoming, so the board fell back on its own resources and began planning a "Citizen's League."

In mid-April Taylor and Gregory had come up with another plan, perhaps learned from the Crowsnest strikes of the previous year. They would form a "non-partisan" group to oppose communism in all its forms wherever it raised its head, particularly in Princeton.

By signing up a mass membership the group would augment (and perhaps disguise) the business owners allied with the management of the Tulameen mine. But a pretence of neutrality was needed: "There is to be no restriction and no qualification other than that its members are sincerely and honestly working for the good of this community"[99]—the not-so-subtle implication being that communists were not working for the good of the community.

Taylor goes on to claim that the creation of the group was "in no sense a class move,"[100] and in fact wasn't even initiated by him and Gregory. No, the move was

> an entirely spontaneous one, and is the consummation of an enquiry which has been quietly proceeding for some time. A definite decision has now been reached, and it has been decided to make a public stand. Public sentiment has been gauged in the fairest and most

thorough manner possible. A special committee has been making an investigation for some time, the method being to secure the views of responsible people of a representative nature. At tonight's meeting all elements were represented; business and professional men, property-holders and laborers, including mine workers. No policy has been laid down and no organization formed, this being left entirely to the public meeting, which will be fully advertised and entirely open.

One thing is agreed, that the situation is serious, and that something must be done if this town is to escape the fate of Fernie.

Fernie, or more generally the Crowsnest Pass mining towns, had recently staged their own seven-month struggle between mine owners and militant coal miners organized in a communist union. There, too, the Klan had burned crosses, police had repeatedly searched miners' houses, and mounted police had clashed with massive picket lines.[101]

The board, with Percy Gregory acting as president and Dave Taylor as secretary, mooted the proposed organization 12 April. Their intentions to combat the imminent threat—not of the owners to close the mine, but of the miners refusing to accept the pay cut—was announced in the *Star* the next day, with a splendid lead paragraph:

> That the time has arrived for the citizens of Princeton to come forward and squarely face what amounts to nothing less than a deliberate attempt to sound the death-knell of this community was the finding of an augmented and representative meeting of the Princeton board of trade tonight.

The town was now back to where it had been at the beginning of the strike in December.

The campaign for the "committee" began in earnest 24 April, and was announced in the paper three days later. What to call it? Clearly Taylor could not decide—he used no less than eight different names in the *Star*, six of them in the same issue: Vigilance Committee, citizens' league, welfare league, Princeton Citizens

League, Princeton Vigilance Association, Vigilance Association, Citizens' Welfare Association, and Welfare Association are each mentioned at one point. We shall call it the Citizens League.

In the 27 April edition some fifty-eight hundred words are spilled on the topic, including the following items:

◆ An article headlined "Citizens Form Vigilance Committee."
◆ An editorial headlined "Testing Time at Hand of Loyalty and Character of Local Citizens: A Time to Stand Together."
◆ A half-page advertisement featuring the illustration on the following page beside copy headlined "It is Your Duty" and "What It Stands For."
◆ An 880-word letter from the president of the miners' union, answered immediately below in a 910-word editorial response.
◆ Three anti-Evans letters.
◆ A short article noting that Evans turned up in Princeton when the miners' cheques arrived.
◆ A further article headlined "Think First Then Act."

In "Citizens Form Vigilance Committee" Taylor claims that the league already comprises two hundred people, with more to come. Its purpose?

> The league has just two planks. These as they are written in the minutes, are "1. To combat the anti-social and communist propaganda being advocated in Canada, notably in the Princeton district. 2. To promote the welfare of the town of Princeton, its industries and its citizens."

The order here is interesting. Two weeks earlier Taylor claimed that the only qualification for membership would be a desire to work for "the good of the community," yet that notion now takes second place to an ideological struggle against those Taylor imagines are disrupting that good. He asks the citizens of Princeton:

> Are you not in favor of these [two planks]? If you are not, you are being classed by your fellow citizens as one who puts Arthur Evans and his professional abuse of honest, well-meaning men ahead of the reputation of these men who serve you out of their own sense

ARE

YOU

A GOOD CITIZEN

• ? •

JOIN THE PRINCETON CITIZENS' LEAGUE

of loyalty to you and your community? [sic] Which is the more reputable, these men or Evans? We are asking you to declare yourself. Your fellow citizens are asking you to say whether you want prosperity or ruin; whether you want Canada or Russia. Have the backbone to declare yourself!

Clearly the real purpose of the league was to coerce the miners into agreeing to the pay cut. Taylor's message throughout the

27 April issue is, "If the miners refuse to take a 10 percent cut the mine will close and the town will die." The questions of the legitimacy of the union, the role played by Evans and the other organizers, the connection to the Soviet Union and International Communism—all are but red herrings. "You must accept the pay cut" is the burden of Taylor's fevered writing.

The Canadian Labour Defence League soon responded to Taylor's hysteria with some of its own. In a leaflet entitled "Community Welfare 'Oh Yeah,'" they demonstrate that they knew perfectly well what the Citizens League true purpose was:

> The Company is broke they say, can't operate unless a wage-cut is accepted, the purpose of this Welfare organization is to put the reduction over, last spring the Miners accepted a 10% reduction, the company promised to return it Sept 1st, did they do it?, it took weeks of organized struggle, in the face of the armed forces of the state to get it back, the reactionary Board of Trade, and the cockroach editor of the Princeton Star-vation rag,worked overtime to accomplish their purpose, with its K.K.Ks and other thugs.

They also alleged the company had a "SPECIALLY PREPARED SET OF BOOKS TO PROVE THEY ARE BROKE," which was probably not far off the mark, given the events a fortnight away.

The anonymous leaflet writer was further incensed by the fact that Taylor and his friends thought of themselves as "the community":

> Let us see who is the Community, is Mr Wagontongue, who garnished numerous Worker's wages just before they were laid off, Workers who had been paying $5.00 per week on back bills, who had been paying cash for their necessities while working, the garnishees costing as high as $16.00 each over and above the amount owed, is McGuffie, the community they speak about, the one who last fall refused the unemployed butter, eggs, ham, or bacon, and would only supply vegetables that were decomposed on their relief slips, is cockroach Taylor, Gregory, Biggs, Naden, Goodfellow and Burr, is this gang of blood sucking bandits the community they speak of?, the real community, in this or any other part of the country are the mass of Worker and Farmers the producers.[102]

The leaflet even addressed Taylor directly, before ending with an uppercase call-to-arms:

> In place of writing epitaphs to Evanskovich and his dupes, you had better get out the crepe, for the burial service of a gang of bloodsucking leaches [sic] who very shortly will have to do some useful task in society, or will not eat.
>
> WORKERS RESIST THE ONSLAUGHT OF THE COMMUNITY WELFARE GANG OF PIRATES. THROUGH ORGANIZATION YOUR WELFARE LIES ... NOT WITH WAGE CUTS OR SPEEDUP.[103]

EIGHT

THE KIDNAPPING

AT SOME POINT after 28 January 1933, Evans was released from prison on bail of ten thousand dollars, conditional on him taking no further part in any strikes or demonstrations in Princeton. Perhaps because of this proviso, Evans redirected his efforts from industrial to political action; on his return to Princeton 7 March he began a political campaign, announced in the *Star* 30 March, to contest the Similkameen seat in the upcoming provincial election, expected in the summer. This would give him the opportunity to make speeches throughout the riding without exposing himself to a charge of contempt of court.

It was in this capacity that he addressed a political meeting in the Britton store in Tulameen on Thursday, 27 April 1933—the same day as the *Star*'s most hysterical issue to date. One particular passage in that issue, in the article headlined "Think First Then Act," seems to foreshadow the evening's events: "A word of caution to our vigilants. So much good has been done that it would be a great pity to spoil it by misdirected zeal." Did Taylor know that Evans was to be kidnapped that night?

Evans later recounted that after the meeting he went to the local home of a Mrs. F. Sandberg for a cup of tea. At about 10:30 p.m. there was a knock at the door—it was Claude Snowden, the local

Ku Klux Klan recruiter. "Evans, come out," he demanded, "we want you." Mrs. Sandberg told Snowden that Evans would have his cup of tea first. Six other men then entered her house and demanded that Evans join them outside. One of the men, Schulli, had a pistol. Mrs. Sandberg told the gunman it was pointing directly at her, and to put it away. After some commotion the strangers took Evans outside, where some twenty-five men were gathered.

Snowden searched Evans and pushed him into one of three waiting cars. Dr. Naden drove Evans's car as the convoy, five men to a car, left Tulameen and headed north towards Merritt. They stopped on several occasions while the men consulted. One such conversation concerned potential trouble at the junction of the Tulameen–Merritt road and the Princeton–Merritt road (now Highway 5A). Buck Allison had heard in Princeton that they might have to battle some "bohunks" there. The rumours proved false, and all three cars stopped at the top of Pearson Hill, overlooking Merritt.

After another consultation, Dr. Naden drove off in the direction of Merritt and the rest of the kidnappers lit a bonfire by the side of the road while Evans remained in the car. Snowden said to him, according to Evans's later testimony, "Down in Arkansas we know how to handle fellows of your description. Don't make any foolish move, because the following car is loaded with shotguns and rifles and those in that car know how to handle them and are prepared to handle them." Dr. Naden returned, and all three cars drove to a flag station on the railway line at Coyle. Evans was put on a train bound for Vancouver.

Evans returned almost immediately—he got off the train at Mission and took the next train back to Princeton. The police took no action whatsoever against the kidnappers, and the attorney general refused to prosecute. Evans launched his own private prosecution and detailed the above account at the preliminary hearing.

The *Star*'s account of the incident, which appeared in its 4 May edition, was naturally very different. Taylor concocted an outrageous justification for what was a clear case of political vigilantism:

> Arthur H. Evans, well known in labor agitations, is not wanted in Princeton. He was told so on Friday night when he was put on the west-bound train, and warned that he would return "at his own risk.". . .
>
> Appeals to the authorities and to the decency of those members of the community who have fallen prey to his wiles being unavailing, a body of picked citizens, including business, professional and labor men, accosted Evans at Tulameen after one of his meetings and told him he was through in this community. He made no protest, and was given transportation on the west-bound train, which he boarded at a point near Merritt. He was advised not to re-appear in Princeton, or send any of his compatriots.

Although Evans had overcome imprisonment and a kidnapping to remain in Princeton, his campaign for the Similkameen seat and preparations for his upcoming section 98 trial—not to mention the conditions of his bail—prevented him from playing a further role in the union struggle.

Fortunately, the mine union leaders had been tested in the fire and now seemed quite capable of looking after themselves—the union had been launched successfully, the contract had been agreed to, and the union had seen to the resignation of the much-disliked John Bennett as superintendent. They now met to formulate a response to the Citizens League more seemly than the "Community Welfare 'Oh Yeah'" leaflet, while nevertheless standing their ground. They decided to take Taylor at his word: a delegation representing the union went to see Taylor, acting in his capacity as secretary of the league. They said that they had noted that the league was in favour of fair play in the dispute, and suggested that the league and the union each select three members to inspect the mine and determine if the miners' safety claims were accurate (the issue of the stoppage of moving coal cars during shift changes still had not been dealt with).

Taylor called a meeting of the league's executive,[104] claiming a public meeting was "impossible as the organization has over two hundred members and a decision was asked for at once."[105] The executive thought the union's safety proposal would not fly, since it required technical knowledge. They did agree, however, to a meeting between the union and the league. Seven men from each group convened in Gregory's office on the evening of Monday, 1 May 1933.

> Mr. Gregory occupied the chair with Mr. Taylor recording, both at the request of the meeting. Also of the citizens' committee were Messrs. E. Barr Hall, (Dr.) J.R. Naden, E.E. Burr, (Rev.) J.C. Goodfellow and W.B. Ewart. For the union were Messrs. E. Plecash, G. Francis, A. Hollands, A. Ryder, S. Lockhart, H. Hayes and J. Cherkosh.[106]

In a special edition of the *Star* published the next evening (Tuesday, 2 May, but misdated Monday, 2 May; see facing page), Taylor outlined what he thought the groups had agreed upon:

> While rigidly adhering to their original demand that no reduction in present rates be tolerated, the miners made definite and important concessions and admissions regarding the conduct of their Union and their relations with the company. On the other hand the citizens came forward with a very clear expression of their attitude with regard to local industry. Points thus established were as follows:
>
> 1. That a definite bond be formed between citizens and employees for the establishment and maintenance of fair working conditions, fair treatment of industry, and community welfare.
> 2. That with regard to the present wage demand, an effort be made to get at the basic principles of the matter; and if at all possible to secure the retention of the present schedule.
> 3. The Union regrets its affiliation with known Communist bodies, but insists that these do not in any way affect the right conduct of its affairs as the employees' organization of the Tulameen mine.
> 4. While considering it inadvisable at this time to make any break from its affiliations, it agrees with the policy of settlement of its own affairs without outside dictation or influence, and approves of a local union supported by and working in harmony with the citizens.

{ Special Edition }

DEDICATED TO SERVICE

The Princeton Star

A Community Paper Published Weekly In The Interests of the Rich and Resourceful Tulameen and Similkameen Valleys

Thirty-Third Year; No. 24.   PRINCETON, B. C., MONDAY, 2nd MAY, 1933 $2.00 Year; 5c Copy.

NEGOTIATIONS MAY SOLVE TULAMEEN ISSUE

MINERS AND CITIZENS WILL MEET DIRECTORS HERE

SETTLEMENT of labor troubles in Princeton appeared to take on new hopes Tuesday morning when following intervention by the newly formed citizens' league the re-opening of the entire matter of the differences between the Tulameen Coal Mines, Ltd., and its employees.

a fair and proper reflex of the bona-fide employees of the company. It insists that only those men actually employed and actually concerned voted, and that they had the opportunity to take a secret ballot but declined. The men insist, however, that under the present working conditions the men cannot accept

...kers of Canada that only active employees had voting privileges. The miners said this had been observed. Only employees voted, and the only employees who did not vote were R. Gray, R. Haddow, J. Leutweyler, E. Hughes, J. Madore, F. Chaisson and W. Worgan. They could have voted had they wished. Mr. Hollands expressed the fear that summer work with the proposed reduction would not be worth while. There was no guarantee of steady work. There was no promise that the cut would be restored. A promise to this effect had been made

recognized Communist organizations and had as their object the overthrow of private ownership and the seizing of control of industry by the masses. As British subjects, the citizens pointed out, they could not endorse such a platform, and could not feel very enthusiastic towards a union which did. Mr. Hall said that the Union had without a doubt been made a medium for the spread of Communistic propaganda. There had been much work of an insidious nature, as for example the Communist Sunday school for the children, which taught disrespect for relig...

5. It insists that outside influences have not dictated its policy in the past, and agrees that they shall not in the future.

6. It repudiates professional agitators of the type of Arthur H. Evans, denies that it is guided by or given encouragement to them, and considers that they are unnecessary and unwelcome in Princeton.

7. It agrees that the seniority clause of the last agreement is unworkable, and surrenders the rights on matters of employment to the manager and the pit committee.

8. It stands willing to take another ballot[107] on the question of the reduction, this time under the supervision of the citizens' committee and by secret ballot.

(By Tuesday evening the ballot had already been arranged; a sidebar elsewhere in the same issue says, "Late this afternoon the *Star* was informed that arrangements had been made for a secret ballot at the mine with regard to the question of the wage reduction. The union has offered this to the mine management, it was stated.")

9. At the same time, it insists that the former decision was a fair and proper reflex of the bona fide employees of the company. It

insists that only those men actually employed and actually concerned voted, and that they had the opportunity to take a secret
ballot but declined.
10. The men insist, however, that under the present working conditions the men cannot accept a wage reduction.
11. That to convince everyone that union meetings were really representative, as stated, the union invited the citizens association
to have two members present at each of its meetings.[108]

Seven of the eleven points concern the internal affairs of the
union; the remaining points (1, 2, 7, and 10) reflect anodyne pos-
itions already known or agreed to. Rather than addressing the
content of the labour dispute before them, Taylor and Gregory
are still obsessed with the question of whether the union properly represented all the striking miners, and none but the striking miners, a question no one else thought relevant.

Taylor, in his special issue, reports Plecash, one of the miners,
as saying

> he was not even interested in Communism, and did not think most
> of the boys had thought much about it in connection with the present
> union. They wanted a union and took the first that was offered them.
> For a number of years, he said, there had been at the Tulameen mine
> a growing oppression of the working man. If an individual protested
> against the conditions he ran the risk of being reported by a "stool-
> pigeon" and being discharged. Last fall the matter of the reduction
> came up, and it was obvious that the same treatment would be meted
> out to those who took the lead in the protest. The first hint he had
> of organization was when he was asked to go to a meeting near the
> Tunnel at night. They got the Scandinavian Hall and decided to ask
> that the ten per cent be restored. A committee was appointed to inter-
> view the management, but got no satisfaction, and the men were
> convinced that it was the manager's plan to stamp out the dissent.
> They did not feel strong enough alone, so they sent out for Mr. Evans.

Taylor responded by saying that he thought miners the very
best of men, and if they had approached either the board of trade
or the *Star* with their complaints, instead of calling for outside

(and, he implied, poisonous) help, they would have listened. He noted in the paper that "several of the miners expressed sympathy with [Taylor's] view. They said that Mr. Evans had had no active part in their union after he had completed its organization. They agreed he was unnecessary now and repudiated him, going on record as so saying."

Taylor clearly thought the miners had been beaten. His new attitude of peace and brotherly love is encapsulated in an editorial in the special issue, headlined "Try Angles":

> And now for our own interpretation of the significance of the developments of this week. We see in them a possible permanent solution to the labor problem in Princeton. It is in the building up of a bond of confidence between miner and citizen. There has been so much genuine goodness displayed by all three elements — miner, employer, and responsible citizen — that we believe that with cool heads we may be able to unite our paths as one.

He was to be disappointed yet again. On Thursday, 4 May, the miners conducted the secret ballot on the question of the 10 percent wage reduction, and voted fifty-seven to six in favour of rejecting the owners' demand. Five days later the owners fulfilled their threat, and closed the mine.

Taylor now had no case to make. He had zealously pursued the communism angle, and failed. The miners knew what the meat of their case was, and on that there would be no compromise. It didn't hurt their cause to say that they had been misled by the dastardly communists, but on the 10 percent reduction they stood firm.

Still, the next issue of the paper, 11 May, featured another anti-Evans letter, and Taylor matched its vitriol with an editorial of some thirty-eight hundred words. He continued his attack on Evans, and took what little solace he could from Evans's "defeat":

> And so Mr. Evans came here and had his little fling. Like any excess, he became unnecessary and nauseating. It takes time to mold public opinion, but when changes have been wrought they are perma-

nent and fair. Thus it worked against Mr. Evans. His stock gradually slumped with those who worshipped him. He reached out with his big stick to make an even bigger hit—and he struck out. The swing of his own abuse and insult recoiled against him. Public decency revolted. Public opinion said Mr. Evans must go. It was too much to expect that he would recognize defeat and leave on his own accord as a public favor. So he was kicked out. He was handled cleanly and firmly, by men whose integrity and intentions are beyond question—men to whom workers are now beginning to realize had their interests at heart. There was no guns, there was no masking, and there was no violence. Nor are the men who took part in the eviction of Mr. Evans hiding their responsibility.

The kidnappers who had so nobly acted on the public's will, according to Taylor—who nevertheless stopped short of publicly naming them—enacted the second act of the Slim Evans kidnapping drama not three weeks after the first. Evans was holding a public meeting at Charles Oland's house in Tulameen on the afternoon of Sunday, 14 May when "twelve to fifteen automobiles drove up . . . [containing] the following passengers: George Murray, Manager of Coalmont collieries, Steve Freeman, J. Ovington, Henry Hopkins, Dave Brydon, E. Canfield, Jack Phillips, A. McEacharn, all of Coalmont Collieries . . . and Percy Gregory, J.J. Biggs, Dr. Nadon [sic], Buck Allison, Harry Allison, Dave Taylor, Stan Garrison, Wm. Fullner, A. Gould," and twenty more men—"all of Princeton B.C."[109]

Gregory again warned Evans not to return to Princeton, and if he did it would be at his own risk. George Murray said, according to Arthur Chisholm, another witness, "Let us take Evans, the son of a bitch, out, and I will make a mulligan of him."[110] No mulligan was made of anyone, and the occasion seems to have petered out.[111] History had repeated itself, but as the German philosopher said, the first time as tragedy, the second as farce.

On 16 May, barely a week after closing the mine, Tulameen Coal Mines Ltd. capitulated to the miners' demands. In a meeting with the union, the Tulameen administration asked for the cancellation of the seniority clause (which the miners had already agreed to), the voiding of the "no Sunday work" clause, and an extension of the old contract to 1 May 1934. The union would not agree. It allowed the already-accepted voiding of the seniority clause, but demanded that until all miners who had been laid off during the past season were rehired, no new men be employed. Regarding work on Sundays, it reluctantly said that it could be discussed on a case-by-case basis. The union rejected the contract extension outright, knowing full well that its bargaining position would be immensely strengthened by negotiating in a time of high coal demand, instead of in the slack summer season. They did undertake, however, to make no new wage demands when the new contract expired 1 January 1935. It was a near-total victory for the miners—the owners and their would-be champion, the *Princeton Star*, had drained the cup of defeat to its bitter dregs.

Perhaps the last word should be left to Taylor. As the commanding general, as it were, of the struggle against the miners, and having been betrayed several times by the very company he had fought for, he nevertheless managed to sound a (mostly) gracious note in his editorial of 18 May 1933, "No Defeat For Us":

> And so we say, congratulations. If everyone is happy, we are. And we might suggest a way to preserve that harmony. While we had thought it looked only possible through a revision of the relationship between the men and the company, we readily admit that the present relationship may suffice if the attitude is amended.
>
> There is only one thing that builds for peace and harmony; and that is a bond of confidence and co-operation. It does not seem to us that the present settlement is inspired by these, but they can grow out of it if both parties are willing. And if they arc thcy will find the citizens more than willing to join with them and makc it a trinity that will build for future happiness. And we maintain that the citizens can do this without changing one iota the outlook they have maintained throughout this controversy.

NINE

THE TRIALS OF SLIM EVANS

SLIM EVANS HAD been charged on 7 December 1932 under section 98 of the Criminal Code. The first of the three charges read: "That Arthur H. Evans . . . did . . . unlawfully advocate, advise, and defend the use, without authority of law, of force as a means of accomplishing a change in the governmental life of Canada"; the other two charges concerned "industrial life" and "economic life." At his preliminary hearing 20 December, he was committed to trial at the spring Assizes in Vernon on 12 June 1933. The prosecutor in both initial appearances was W.H. Bullock-Webster, the Crown's chief legal advisor and a man with a history of police work (he had been chief constable of the Kootenay district and was well experienced with striking miners in Rossland). By the date of the trial, some forty-three thousand people had signed a petition to the provincial government asking for the withdrawal of the charges against Evans.[112]

Evans was not alone in Vernon. Many workers had travelled by freight to be there; the *Unemployed Worker* reported that at a Workers' Defence Conference in Vancouver 28 May, a "workers' jury" had been selected to travel to Vernon and witness the trial. On their arrival they sought a meeting with Judge W.A. McDonald, presented him with a document outlining their demands, and requested he guarantee them seating in the court-room gallery during the trial.

> The document . . . took note how distinguished guests were fre-quently granted special places in court merely to satisfy their idle curiosity as to court procedure, and that the workers' jury had in this instance a thousand times more right to a similar courtesy of a special place in court.

The astonished judge said that "if the workers jury would give their names to the Sheriff at Vernon he would instruct the Sheriff to see that they were seated."

The trial opened with Evans protesting the jury pool. As the *Unemployed Worker* noted,

> The prosecutor was compelled to read Evans' affidavit of Prejudice protesting against a deliberately framed up jury.[113] It was quite appar-ent when we looked that jury over that there were not nearly enough jurors there to compose the complete panel of 48 as required by the Jurors' Act. Also that the occupation and mien of those jurors was not such that would guarantee a fair trial—their visages portrayed ignorance egotism and degeneration. . . .
>
> The air was tense. Briefs dropped to the table—bulls fidgeted—dis-engaged Counsel gawked in dismay and it was very apparent that the Judge wanted a six foot hole to open up and swallow him.[114]

Evans was perfectly correct—the jury pool was deficient, and the case was "stood over" for three months.

In the meantime, the trial of Evans's kidnappers went ahead—but it, too, became a comedy of errors. Crown counsel and the attor-ney-general ignored what should have been a state prosecution on an open-and-shut case, and so it was up to Evans and his lawyer, Gordon Grant, who had represented the Canadian Labour Defense League in a number of court battles, to put the case together.

Grant delayed filing a charge in the kidnapping until 9 June. Summonses to appear were first reported in the *Star* of

15 June, and a preliminary hearing was set for the following day in Merritt. The case was heard by H.G. Hooper, a justice of the peace in Nicola, "who has not heard a case in several months," reported Taylor. "No active justice in the district would accept the case." Hooper adjourned the case to Saturday, 24 June back in Princeton.[115]

The Princeton hearing, before magistrate L.A. Dodd (who, it will be remembered, had been the target of the march of 30 November 1932 and the recipient of the unemployed workers' list of grievances), was adjourned again until 30 June. A hearing was finally arranged for 6 July at Coalmont, again before Hooper, who dismissed the case due to the lack of attendance of either Evans or Grant. Two of the accused, Snowden and Fuller, had not even been served with summonses.[116]

Dave Taylor, as secretary of the board of trade, and E.E. Burr, owner of the Burr Garage, and perhaps others, then launched a campaign to stop the proceedings. Their letters to the attorney-general prompted this reply:

> I quite appreciate the situation and feelings of the citizens of your district and elsewhere in connection with the above named. In a proper case, of course, as Attorney-general I could order the proceedings to be stopped, but in this case, when you consider the situation, do you not think it would be inadvisable and no doubt indiscreet on my part to exercise the power vested in me? While it might be justifiable, yet the effect would be that this rampant individual would proclaim from the housetops how "a capitalistic, tyrannical government impeded the wheels of justice." It is not desirable to give him this ammunition to fire off.[117]

On 27 July, Taylor reported that Evans and Grant had filed a new charge "alleg[ing] forcible imprisonment," and "a joint charge of conspiracy was also filed, but was not proceeded with." A hearing was set for 1 August 1933 in Coalmont, before Justice of the Peace Norman Craigie. Our record of the trial consists of transcripts of Evans's examination by Grant; his cross-examinations, by Woodward on behalf of the two policemen accused, and by Shaw on behalf of the other accused; and of course Taylor's account in the *Star* of 3 August.

Inexplicably, the eight defendants named in Evans's suit did not include Dr. Naden, who knew full well that Evans was being kidnapped, or Schulli, who allegedly held the gun. The eight accused were Constables Hatherill and Miller of the B.C. Provincial Police, Percy Gregory, Stephen Freeman, William Fuller, Stanley Garrison (stable boss at Pleasant Valley Mine), Claude Snowden (one of the men in the tombstone photograph on page 65; he is listed as a miner in the 1932 *Directory* but disappears henceforth, and did not appear for the trial), and Buck Allison (who was noted for his physical size and strength. as well as his "well-known campaign for clearing Canada of aliens. He walked down the sidewalk where the Russians stand and at each group he would ask, 'Are you a Bohunk or are you not??' If they answered 'yes', he hit them and if they merely looked unpleasant and said nothing, he kicked them"[118]). The Star described the defendants first as "known and highly respected local laborers, business men and professional men,"[119] and later as "prominent local men."[120]

NO REGRETS!

An illustration from the 20 September 1933 issue of *Unemployed Worker*.

The defence argued that no violence was threatened or inflicted, and that Evans was persuaded to leave town voluntarily. It made perfect sense to the kidnappers that they represented all that was best in Princeton, and thus had the right to decide who was and was not an asset to the community.

The cross-examinations of Evans were mostly concerned with testing his believability, initially by excursions into his arrest and conviction in Alberta. Evans had been convicted of fraudulent conversion of monies held by him in trust as district secretary of the One Big Union, and sentenced to three year's prison, of which he served nine months—he was released following a petition signed by eight thousand miners. Further cross-examination was more relevant to the section 98 trial Evans would face later in the year; Grant successfully objected to these questions, but the cross-examinations as a whole were nevertheless damaging to the case.

We do not know if the charges were dismissed or whether the accused were all acquitted, as they would have been had they given any evidence.[121] Taylor reported that due to Evans's "unbelief" in God his testimony was "technically ruled out," though we can't be certain that this was the case. We do not know whether Evans and Grant considered an appeal. The *Star* reported that

> the justice of the peace said that much of the prosecution was evidently unsatisfactory. Nothing had been substantially proven to confirm the charge, and he did not feel justified in putting the accused to needless worry and expense on such grounds.
>
> Mr. Woodward stated that he would recommend that a charge of conspiracy be laid against Evans and his associates in connection with the charges brought against the police.[122]

The failure of Evans and Grant to put together a stronger case granted Evans's enemies a court victory in addition to their claimed moral superiority. Dave Taylor now had legal backing to his thirty-eight hundred words from 11 May justifying the kidnapping and proclaiming to the world, from the rooftops of Princeton, that these "principled" men had done nothing wrong.

★

Evans's section 98 trial finally got under way on the morning of 14 September 1933. Grant began by arguing that Evans be allowed to cross-examine the witnesses and address the jury, and Grant would make any relevant legal points. Judge MacDonald assented.

The first witness was Constable William Thomson of the B.C. Provincial Police. He testified that he first met the defendant 13 September 1932, when Evans was addressing a meeting of coal miners at night in the open air—this was the first meeting of miners but the police were already surveilling Evans and planning for the eventuality of a strike. Thomson then reported on each of the meetings Evans had spoken at, describing the miners as "Yugo-Slavs, Czecho-Slavs, Servians, some Russians, English, Scotch—the southern Europeans in predominance." He testified that Evans sang at a couple of the meetings, notably "The Internationale" and "Should I Ever Be a Soldier."[123] In cross-examination, Thomson admitted that he had pressured the owner of the Tulameen hall, a Mr. Johnson, not to rent to Evans and the miners.

Other police witnesses followed, including Sergeant Duncan, who had participated on 2 December 1932 when the police had forcibly broken up the picket line with horses and clubs. Evans cross-examined them on various matters, such as their definition of the word "force."

At the end of the Crown's case Grant moved for a directed verdict (meaning the case would be dismissed), arguing that the evidence given did not constitute an offence. The judge, however, disagreed,and so Evans called his witnesses. They included H.F. Hayes, president of the miners' union, and several witnesses of the events of 2 December 1932, when the police had forcibly broken up the picket line with horses and clubs.

The judge's summation noted that what the trial came down to was whether Evans had taught, advocated, advised or defended the use of force in any manner (repeating the words "in any manner"). He warned the jury at some length that it was not for them

Workers defend the Evans home in Vancouver, April 1934. The placards read "Picket Line on Com. Evans Home Organise & Fight" (top) and "Evans is in for us. We're out for him."

to consider whether section 98 was a good law or a bad law; were they to do that, he said, "you would be disobeying the oath you took as jurors, when you swore that you would render a verdict according to the evidence."

After praising Sergeant Duncan as a "quiet, reasonable man," Judge MacDonald repeated Duncan's account of Evans prais-

ing Russian practices at one of the meetings, then addressed the jury: "Now, do you consider, if you accept that evidence, that that was advocacy of the system which is now in vogue in Russia—would present Russia as a better place for workers than our Dominion?" He repeated more of Duncan's testimony, in which Evans had said, in Duncan's words, "it was only by fighting that reforms he was advocating could be brought about, and said that the blood of the workers had been smeared in the streets of the chief cities of the capitalistic worlds, and would be quite likely spilt in Princeton."

Again the judge asked the jury: "If you accept that would you accept that as advocating physical force? It is for you to say." He then instructed the jury to consider who Evans was addressing, and how it would be construed:

Would it be construed that "force" was to be force of argument, or was it to be a force that, I think I am safe in instructing you, meant physical force of some kind—not discussing the matter with the government, or its officials—but endeavouring to accomplish, what was accomplished in Russia, through a Soviet Government—through communism?[124]

After such a summation the verdict was a foregone conclusion. The jury took seventy minutes to find Evans guilty on all three charges. He was sentenced to one year imprisonment. The *Star*'s reporting on this was the last item to appear on Evans or the strike.[125] Evans filed an appeal, and bail was again refused. In March 1934 the appeal failed, and in a last act of vindictiveness, the appeal court ruled that the one-year sentence would commence on the day the appeal failed, thus sentencing Evans to an effective eighteen months imprisonment, since he had been in jail from September 1933 to March 1934.

The authorities had still not finished with Evans and his family. Since he was now in prison he was automatically barred from running in the upcoming provincial election. And because he could not work he could not make payments on his mortgage; the mortgage holder, Vancouver alderman W.J. Twiss, soon began proceedings to evict Evans's wife and child from their home. Many workers rallied to defend the home, but on 24 April 1934, "twenty carloads of police swept down in a surprise attack, assisted by eight police on horseback, six motor cycle police and the chief of police. In all 150 police participated—all this to evict one mother and her seven year old child."[126]

TEN

THE AFTERMATH

THE CRISIS OF capitalism called the Great Depression shook many foundations, not the least of which was electoral politics. In August 1928 the Conservative Party, led by Simon Tolmie, had defeated the incumbent Liberals to form British Columbia's government. Tolmie and the province enjoyed a full year of prosperity before the Wall Street collapse of October 1929, a shock neither Tolmie nor most of his cabinet understood. As historian S.W. Jackman notes,

> The incompetence of the Tolmie government was evident to all for the Premier and his colleagues did nothing. The few able men in the cabinet resigned and were replaced by persons even more reactionary and even less experienced. . . . Tolmie was completely out of his depth in the crisis that he had to face.[127]

Tolmie tried to form a coalition government, but the Liberals and their new leader, Duff Pattullo, would not hear of it.

Tolmie's comeuppance arrived with the provincial election of November 1933. The Conservative Party was wiped out: it declined even to run candidates, and only a handful of "Conservatives" were elected, under various banners. The Liberals and Patullo, campaigning on a platform of "Work and Wages," elected thirty-four MLAs (including Charles Tupper for the Similkameen, the seat Evans had sought but was unable to contest by virtue of being in jail).[128] The new Co-operative Commonwealth Federation (CCF) became, with seven seats, the Official Opposition. The only government members to survive were former attorney general Robert Pooley (who had sent the B.C. Provincial Police into Princeton), running as a Unionist, and Clive Montgomery, Francis Planta, and Rolf Wallgren Bruhn, who were re-elected as members of the Non Partisan Independent Group.

Much the same occurred federally in 1935, when William Lyon Mackenzie King and the Liberal Party massively defeated R.B. Bennett's Conservative government, 171 seats to 39. That election saw the disappearance of the Progressive Party and the United Farmers of Alberta, and the birth of two new federal parties: the CCF with seven seats and the Social Credit Party with seventeen.

In 1935 the Tulameen mine was nearing its "best before" date. By then most of the coal being worked lay under the Tulameen River, necessitating a great deal of pumping. The minister of mines reported that

> operations were suspended during the month of February [1935]; the mine allowed to fill with water, and no further work was done until the autumn, when arrangements were again made to place this mine in operation. This recovery-work commenced during the early part of September, but due to the inflow of water and extremely heavy caving of the underground roadways the ventilation had not been restored at the end of the year.[129]

Early in 1936 the mine was up and running again, but only briefly: in March it was again filled with water.

The local branch of the Mine Workers' Union of Canada protested. "The closing down of Princeton's main industry is the means of throwing out of employment 160 workers, cessation of the major part of the community's payroll," reads a piece of CLDL campaign literature. "It will result in the transformation of Princeton into a GHOST TOWN."[130] But this time the threat of closure was not a mere bargaining chip—1936 was the Tulameen mine's last year of operation.

The focus of labour activities in Princeton thereafter shifted from the coal mines to the several relief camps in the area. An RCMP Secret Report of 18 April 1935 noted that

> on 6th April, approximately 450 relief camp strikers, members of the Relief Camp Workers' Union, gathered at Princeton, B.C. from the surrounding camps and stopped and boarded a passenger train demanding transportation to Vancouver. The Canadian Pacific Railway agent at Princeton promised to make a request to head office to supply an engine and box cars to carry them to their destination. In view of this promise the strikers withdrew from the train. The station agent's request was refused however, and as a result the strikers boarded the next freight train outside the Princeton city limits and arrived in Vancouver on the morning on the 9th.[131]

Was it merely a coincidence that Arthur Evans had recently been released from Oakalla after serving nine months of his sentence? An RCMP report of 9 January 1935 noted that he was on a speaking tour of B.C., with dates scheduled up and down the coast and throughout the Interior. "He is due to speak in Princeton 1 January 1935," the RCMP reported.[132] Engagements later that month took him to Valemount and McBride, and to Prince Rupert on 3 February. At this last venue, before some three hundred people, he told of his arrest in Princeton and his experiences in Oakalla jail. He gave this account again at a meeting 15 February—in the Victoria chamber of commerce, no less.[133]

Though transients were constantly moving around the country on freight trains looking for work, the trend was to move west, where the climate was more salubrious. Now the idea arose for a move eastwards. The relief camp workers and others wanted to put pressure on Ottawa to do more to help the unemployed, and so the "On To Ottawa Trek" was devised. Slim Evans was its main organizer.

✳

"A spectre is haunting Europe," wrote Marx and Engels in 1848, "the spectre of communism." Though their projection was somewhat premature, it did indeed haunt the whole of the short twentieth century, 1914–1991. Opinions about the Soviet Union, the Revolution, and communism—international and national—defined one politically. The struggle for and against communism defined the century, and in 1932–33 manifested itself in a small industrial town in western Canada.

Ostensibly, the conflict in Princeton was about a strike arising from a broken promise. But because the miners called in an organizer who was a communist, it was never a simple economic strike; there was always more in the picture. In the eyes of many workers, capitalism had created the boom-and-bust cycle, and thus capitalism was responsible for the miseries of the masses. Slim Evans was one of a number of these workers who saw in the hopelessness of the Great Depression a lever to change the course of history.

Only fifteen years earlier the Russians had transformed the largest country in the world into a workers' state. The Soviet Union was building a new society, and millions throughout North America, worn down by the depression and the hopelessness of any visible capitalist solution, wanted to share in its prospects. Here was an end to capitalism's endless creed of "more," its contradiction of starvation in the midst of plenty, its transformation of working-class people into a mere element of production to be disposed of when not needed. The socialist homeland had lifted millions out of poverty with (what seemed at the time) a howlingly successful planned economy, and inspired an international communist movement.

In Canada in the 1920s and '30s communists were the only organized segment of the working class that took the struggle to the enemy; it was natural that their popularity grew during the depression. The Communist Party's job, as its members saw it, was to "fan the flames of discontent"(to borrow the Wobbly's phrase) and to encourage enough interest and enthusiasm to incite the revolution. The energy one sees in every issue of the *Unemployed Worker* is testimony to the success of the communist ticket in those years.

But the movement also had a vulgar element. Communist writers, while trying to present and delineate that energy, tended towards sensational and shocking, often nature-based language, describing their opponents with phrases like "fascist insect" and "running dog," words such as "lickspittle" and "cockroach." The words were intended to give workers, many of whom had come from cultures where deference to the boss or the policeman was automatic and unthinking, the moral courage to take a stand. "Your opponents," the writer would say, "are not your betters or your superiors; they are not even your equals. They are a lower form of life and you should think of them in that way." This rhetoric prompted strong reactions from those who, like Dave Taylor and Percy Gregory, recognized themselves as the enemy identified by the communists.

Taylor and Gregory had already internalized their ideological belief that the coming of communism would be an unmitigated disaster. It was the task of Evans and his fellow workers to provide a counterweight to that view, to imbue the miners with a sense of destiny—and that is precisely what they did in Princeton. Evans was concerned about the material well-being of workers both employed and unemployed, and was successful in helping to unify the miners and demonstrate the strength in union. But his long-term goal was to raise the workers' consciousness, to help them understand the roots of the depression, the likes of which no one had ever experienced. To those tossed about in the waves of the economic crisis his message must have inspired hope: "If people create problems, then they can also solve them."

Taylor knew this message resonated with many, and what that portended. Economically speaking, perhaps he should have realized that neither he nor Gregory, a real estate salesman and surveyor, were economically threatened by a successful strike; the more money the miners made, the more the town (and their own businesses) would prosper. But Taylor was haunted by the spectre of communism, especially since capitalism seemed to be caving in around his ears, and so he cast in his lot with the "oppressor"—which probably worked against his own interests in a town composed mostly of miners.

Taylor's anti-communist hysteria—there is unfortunately no better word for it—got the better of him, and led him in directions that were antithetical to the town's progress. The rhetoric in the pages of the *Princeton Star* (like that engendered in other struggles—one thinks of the American South's reaction to the Civil Rights movement) identified an Other, an alien force coming to wreak havoc on the community. But how could one organizer and a couple of sidekicks take over a town? Was the Kremlin really planning to conquer the world, starting with Princeton? To Taylor these things seemed possible, if not likely. He saw his role in Princeton as a Cassandra, and that was his tragedy. Where he saw disaster, others saw hope. He saw no remedy for the state of affairs in Princeton; his only hope was to restore the status quo ante; and in the 1930s, that was not enough. He spoke and wrote as if he believed his and the miners' interests were one and the same, equally threatened by the communists, but his actions belied his rhetoric. His rabid and insensate opposition led him to some dark places, and in the process, he said things and committed acts he possibly later regretted.

Taylor and Gregory both left the board of trade in January 1934; there is no record of either participating in political work thereafter. We know nothing of Gregory's trajectory after the strike other than that he remained in Princeton and carried on his business. He died in 1953.

Dave Taylor stayed on as proprietor and editor of the *Star* until 1939, but seems to have withdrawn from public life. In 1936 he began publishing poems he had written. Some nineteen of them appeared in the *Star* between 1936 and 1939, and another six appeared in 1946.[134] In March 1939 Taylor sailed to Nanking and found work as a feature writer for the *Manchuria Daily News*. He later worked as chief reporter on the *Shanghai Times*, and in August 1941 as news editor for the *Singapore Herald*. He then travelled to Britain. In an article he wrote about himself in 1950 he said that

> on arrival in Britain he was called to the War Office by the Intelligence Service and was later consultant for the *London Daily Express* on Far Eastern affairs. In support of honest loyalty he served well in the Shanghai Volunteers and the Royal Fusiliers as a private.[135]

He returned to Princeton in 1946 and took over the editing of the *Star* from Rev. John Goodfellow. Over the next few years the frequency and regularity of the paper diminished. Taylor became somewhat of a "character" around town, and a bit of a recluse. He died in 1986.

Slim Evans lived a life of personal and political struggle, and died in harness. The 1935 On to Ottawa Trek made it as far as Regina, where a deal was struck: the striking workers would remain behind, watched by a large contingent of RCMP officers, while a delegation of eight, including Evans, went to Ottawa to meet with Prime Minister R.B. Bennett. The meeting, which lasted an hour, was one of the most dramatic events of the Thirties, with the champions of the left and the right duking it out. Bennett called Evans a thief; Evans retorted by calling Bennett a liar. The situation on Evans's return to Regina grew desperate, and culminated in a massive police-provoked riot on Dominion Day 1935. The subsequent inquiry contributed to the eventual reform of the relief camp system. Evans returned to B.C. and continued his labour activism. He was in Vancouver returning home from an Amalgamated Building Workers convention in February 1944 when he was struck by a car and died.[136] He was fifty-three years old.

Throughout the rest of the century, Princeton remained at the mercy of one or two large industries, whether copper mining or logging, and remains today what it has always been—a mining town in a farming and ranching environment. More recently it has achieved a more stable economic base, aided by a steady stream of folks retiring from pensioned work on the coast. The mines in question have turned from coal to copper, but still the town's fortunes largely depend upon commodity prices set in distant markets. If copper goes up a few cents the town is crawling with new four-by-fours; a few cents down and the mine closes, with all the attendant social upheavals: sliding real estate prices, closing schools, and the bankruptcy of ancillary businesses.

What has saved Princeton from becoming a ghost town—as was the fate of so many mining towns founded in the south of B.C.'s Interior at the turn of the twentieth century—was, paradoxically, farming and ranching. The farmers and ranchers always saw themselves as committed and stable, and viewed the mining sector as uncommitted, unstable, and peopled by aliens with no sense of loyalty to the town It was the alternate economy provided by farming and ranching that allowed Princeton to weather the lean years and remain a mining town to this day.

The Copper Mountain mine, just south of town, operated until 1996 and then reopened in 2011, but the nearly four hundred employees there today (one could scarcely call them "miners") have exerted only a minor cultural or political impact on the town. They have certainly not yet integrated themselves into Princeton's permanent community to the extent that the "footloose" 1930s miners did.

Today Princeton's collective memory of the events of the 1930s are fast disappearing; few even know that Princeton itself was once a mining site. With the memories of those clamorous years living on in fewer and fewer lives, this book has been an attempt to make sense of what they experienced.

ENDNOTES

CHAPTER 1: PRINCETON, 1932

1. This was why the ranchers wanted to maintain the unincorporated status of the town, which made it unique in B.C.'s southern interior. It did not incorporate until 1951; the campaign to incorporate was led by a miner.

2. 1891 Census of Canada, District Yale, Sub-District Princeton, Library & Archives Canada, http://www.bac-lac.gc.ca/eng/census/1891/Pages/about-census.aspx.

3. The 1890 B.C. *Directory* for "Princeton" lists some fifty-five names, including two First Nations, but no Chinese names at all, suggesting a total population of perhaps 140.

4. The town properly dates from this period, despite the highway signs indicating "Princeton, est. 1860."

5. All figures from the *Annual Report of the Minister of Mines of British Columbia* (Victoria: British Columbia Department of Mines, 1925–1939).

6. "Production and productivity, Tulameen Coal Mines Ltd.," 1924–1935; from *Annual Report of the Minister of Mines, 1924–1935*.

7. Of the forty-five men who were killed in the Blakeburn Mine disaster of 1930, fully twenty-two had Eastern European names: see the 1930 *Annual Report*.

8. Herbert Hoover, *The Memoirs of Herbert Hoover, Vol 3: The Great Depression* (London: Hollis and Carter, 1952), 30.

9. More properly, *I. W. W. Songs to Fan the Flames of Discontent*, which

went through an astonishing twenty-four editions before 1932.

10. *Workers' Unity League: Policy, Tactics, Structure, Demands* (Toronto: WUL National Office, n.d., ca. 1932). Quoted in Stephen Lyon Endicott, *Raising the Workers' Flag: The Workers' Unity League of Canada, 1930–1936* (Toronto: University of Toronto Press, 2012), ix.

11. British Columbia Legislative Assembly, *Annual Report of the Department of Labour for the Year Ended December 1932* (Victoria: 1933).

12. Endicott, 27.

13. M. Allerdale Grainger, *Riding the Skyline Trail* (Victoria: Horsdal & Schubart, 1994), 95.

14. Grainger, 85.

CHAPTER 2: SLIM EVANS COMES TO PRINCETON

15. Evidence of Constable William Thomson, *Rex v. Arthur Herbert Evans*, Adjourned Spring Assizes, Vernon, September 1933, before Mr. Justice W.A. Macdonald and jury, p. 7 of trial transcript.

16. Jean Evans Sheils and Ben Swankey, *Work and Wages! Semi-Documentary Account of the Life and Times of Arthur H. (Slim) Evans* (Vancouver: Trade Union Research Bureau, 1977), 6.

17. The Colorado National Guard and guards from the Colorado Fuel & Iron Company opened fire on a camp of striking miners and their families, killing twenty-four people, including women and children.

18. Biographical information from evidence of the complainant Arthur Herbert Evans in *Rex v. Gregory et al.*, Coalmont, BC, August 1933, before Norman Craigie, Justice of the Peace.

19. By this point Evans was already being monitored by the local provincial constable Thomson, who had advised the owner of the hall not to rent it to Evans: *Rex v. Arthur Herbert Evans*, 5, 16.

20. Endicott, 154; *Rex v. Arthur Herbert Evans*, 39.

21. Endicott, 155.

22. Meetings were held 17 November at the Scandinavian Hall; 18 November, Orange Hall; 19 November, I.O.O.F. Hall; 22 November, Orange Hall; 23 November, Princess Theatre (a smoker, at which Evans sang "Should I Ever Be a Soldier" and "The Internationale"); 24 November, I.O.O.F. Hall (a wedding, with Evans again singing "The Internationale" and, with others, "The Cops'll Have a Hell of a Time" and "They are Filling the Town with Bulls"; 29 November and 6 December, Workers' Centre. All dates from *Rex v. Arthur Herbert Evans*, 5–13.

23. It should not be forgotten that the miners were not ethnically homogenous—though miners of British extraction were perhaps the

largest group, they did not constitute a majority, and Eastern European miners (mostly of German and Slavic origins) speaking a variety of languages made up a large proportion of Princeton miners.

24. *Princeton Star*, 1 December 1932.

25. From various issues of the *Star*: "well informed men of reasonable views"; "thinking citizens, devoted to the welfare of the community"; "reasonably minded people"; "broad-minded person(s)"; "rational citizens"; "the responsible citizens"; "sincere men."

26. Cross examination of Constable William Thomson in *Rex v. Arthur Herbert Evans*, 52–54.

27. Much of this information is drawn from the B.C. Directories published in Vancouver, mostly on a yearly basis until 1948, with the exceptions of 1906–1909 and 1911–1917. The Gregory family is listed in the 1921 Census.

28. Laurie Currie, *Princeton 120 Years* (Princeton, B.C.: Similkameen Spotlight Publishing, 1990), 79.

29. Information about Taylor is drawn from Nicholas Mills, *Once Upon a Time in Princeton* (Chilliwack, B.C.: self-published, 2013).

CHAPTER 3: TROUBLE AT THE MINES

30. *Princeton Star*, 1 December 1932; *Unemployed Worker*, 3 December 1932.

31. Remembered some thirty years later by Art Hewitt and collected by B.C. song collector Phil Thomas, 22 August 1970: Philip J. Thomas Song Collection, Aural History Archives, Royal B.C. Museum & Archives, item #120.

32. According to the *Star*, the song "was not set to the music of Beethoven or Mozart, nor even to the battle-inspired air of the Marseillaise but to the immortal tune of 'Inky Pinky Parlez-Vous.' Though the police deny that it discomfited them in any way, it was one of the bases for the charge. The other was a generally hostile and defiant attitude which the defendant assumed when the people attempted to disperse the band, alleged leader of the entire disturbance, and without a doubt the musical tetrarch, for in addition to supplying the air and the words, he also, according to the police, went through all the motions of the leader of a full-fledged symphony."

33. Evidence of Constable Duncan: *Rex v. Arthur Herbert Evans*, 101.

34. Evidence of Mary Kraetor and Nancy Lukow: *Rex v. Arthur Herbert Evans*, 158, 162.

35. *Princeton Star*, 8 December 1932.

36. Or possibly the same morning—Evans's letter claims three

a.m. on the sixth, but the *Star* reported the arrest took place at ten a.m. on the seventh.

37. The *Unemployed Worker* (24 December 1932) claimed that Driscoll was charged with the same offence, for "holding a meeting in a slave camp where the workers are sleeping on the floor, not being allowed to make bunks, working on an air port, 20¢ a day of 8 hours." The same paper the next week (31 December) reported that he had been sentenced to forty-two days hard labour, so clearly the s. 98 charge was dropped or never laid.

38. From a letter to the paper from Evans, *Unemployed Worker*, 17 December 1932.

39. Quite who these "well-informed men of reasonable views," a group frequently referred to, consisted of, was never made exactly clear, though it certainly included Dave Taylor, and probably also included Percy Gregory. These two appear to have imagined themselves, in the absence of a town council (since Princeton was still unincorporated) an informal senate. *Star*, 8 December 1932.

40. *Star*, 15 December 1932.

41. Ibid.

42. Ibid.

43. Ibid.

44. F.E. Harrison, "Preliminary Report to Deputy Minister of Labour," Ottawa, 15 December 1932.

CHAPTER 4: TROUBLE AT THE LABOUR CAMPS

45. McNaughton Papers, cited in Louise Gwenyth Gorman, "State Control and Social Resistance: The Case of the Department of National Defence Relief Camp Scheme in B.C." (master's thesis, University of British Columbia, 1985), 90.

46. James H. Gray, *The Winter Years* (Toronto: Macmillan of Canada, 1966), 147–48.

47. Gorman, 97

48. Endicott, 90

49. H. Dew, "The Relief Camp Bane," in James Skitt Matthews, "Unemployment and Relief," Additional Manuscripts 54, vol. 8, no. 3 (May 1935), Vancouver City Archives, quoted in Gorman, 103.

50. *Princeton Star*, 26 January 1933.

51. Ibid., 20 April 1933.

52. Referred to throughout this book as "Driscoll."

53. Lowe had been arrested, charged and jailed for vagrancy (three months in Oakalla jail) 27 February 1933: *Unemployed Worker*,

1 March 1933.

54. Cross examination of Constable William Thomson in *Rex v. Arthur Herbert Evans*, 52–54.

55. The *Unemployed Worker* in Vancouver also followed this course of political action, establishing neighbourhood councils to assist members with problems of overdue rent, unsafe apartments, and government neglect or cruelty—thus assuring workers that when they stood against any type of authority, they did not stand alone.

56. The Immigration Act allowed for the swift deportation of offenders, and was often invoked to threaten politically conscious workers born outside Canada. Between 1930 and 1935, an estimated thirty thousand immigrants were summarily deported, usually for being a public charge: see "Forging Our Legacy: Canadian Citizenship and Immigration, 1900–1977," Citizenship and Immigration Canada website (http://www.cic.gc.ca/english/resources/publications/legacy/chap-4b.asp#chap4-9).

57. Taylor's error: section 98 concerns overthrowing the government by force, and was the section with which Evans would be charged. As to sections 41 and 42 of the Immigration Act: "During the Depression years, Canada increasingly resorted to deportation as a means to remove 'undesirable' immigrants from Canadian soil. According to the *Immigration Act*, an immigrant could be deported for any one of several reasons: criminality; medical reasons; immoral behaviour; illegal entry to Canada; becoming a public charge or advocating the overthrow of the government by force." From Vadim Kukushkin, "Shipped Out," in *Moving Here Staying Here: The Canadian Immigrant Experience*, Collections Canada website (http://www.collectionscanada.gc.ca/immigrants/021017-2520-e.html).

58. This demand calls to mind (and was perhaps worded by someone familiar with) a verse from "Fifty Thousand Lumberjacks," a well-known IWW song from the 1917 strike:

> *Take a tip and start right in; plan some cozy rooms / Six or eight spring beds in each, with towels, sheets, and brooms, / Shower baths for men who work keep them well and fit, / A laundry, too, and drying room would help a little bit.*

In *IWW Songs to Fan the Flames of Discontent*, 13th ed. (Chicago: Industrial Workers of the World, 1917). The song had appeared in full in the *Similkameen Star*, 29 August 1919, during a strike by Similkameen loggers.

59. *Unemployed Worker*, 24 December 1932.

60. Although the *Star* of 29 December 1932 says only seventeen men walked out.

61. Driscoll was sentenced to forty-two days' hard labour at Oakalla Prison in Burnaby: *Princeton Star*, 29 December 1932.

62. *Princeton Star*, 26 January 1933.

63. Ibid., 2 February 1933.

64. *Unemployed Worker*, 8 March 1933.

CHAPTER 5: FIERY CROSSES AND BEATINGS IN THE NIGHT

65. *Star*, 22 December 1932

66. *Unemployed Worker*, 24 December 1932

67. Julian Sher, *White Hoods: Canada's Ku Klux Klan* (Vancouver: New Star Books, 1983), 19. Sher goes on to note that "by 1927, the Klan claimed a BC membership of 13,000, including 8,000 in Vancouver and 3,000 in Victoria" and that "fueling the Klan fires burning in BC was the anti-immigrant phobia then reigning in the province." (p.32).

68. Kyle Franz, "One Flag, One School, One Language: The Ku Klux Klan and the Crowsnest Pass, 1932," *Heritage News* no. 3, 15 July 2010. The RCMP's predilection for the political right rather than the left is indicated by the description of these Klan members as "good citizens."

69. Endicott, 117.

70. Claude Snowden was a Tulameen miner, and appears in the photograph of the fake gravestone on page 65. "Hughey" may refer to John Huey, master mechanic at Tulameen Coal Mines Ltd. Prideaux was an agent of Confederation Life, and later a leading opponent of the town's incorporation. The Burrs were the garage owner and his sons. "Leatherby" may be Herbert Letherbe, a clerk at C.V. Prosser, the local harness store. Of the others we found no extant records.

71. The resignation of Bennett must have gladdened many a union heart. A song about him was still recalled in 1970 when it was collected from Art Rider by Phil Thomas. It was set to the tune of "Ìvan Skavinsky Skavar," and ran:

> There's a mine in the west where the Tulameen flows / Where they're digging out coal by the day/But the methods they use and the amount of abuse is driving the miners away. // John Bennett was head of that Tulameen spread / And Bill Strang was boss down the mine; / John Bennett was known as a son of a bitch / And Bill was a dirty old swine (P.J. Thomas Collection #121).

Bill Strang, the overman at no. 2 mine, died early the following year in a mine accident (*Annual Report of the Minister of Mines for the Year 1935*, p. G9).

72. December 1933; Arthur Evans Fonds, Special Collections, University of British Columbia.

73. *Unemployed Worker*, 21 January 1933.

74. *Princeton Star*, 26 January 1933.

75. *Unemployed Worker*, 21 January 1933; *Star*, 19 and 26 January 1933.

76. *Unemployed Worker*, 15 February 1933. The presence of an anti-union song is intriguing—perhaps the right had learned something from the left.

77. The remaining members of the 1932 board of trade, possibly among the "unknown" men in the photo, are J.G. Biggs, the provincial mine inspector; Walter L. Boult, sub-collector of customs; Victor G. Field, manager of the Bank of Montreal; Rev. J.C. Goodfellow (not pictured, according to his son); H.G. McDonald, of the Cosmopolitan Store; and H.C. McGuffie, proprietor of Princeton Cash Store.

Chapter 6: Unlawful Associations

78. Richard Fidler, "Proscribing Unlawful Associations: The Swift Rise and Agonizing Demise of Section 98" (paper submitted to Prof. Douglas Hay, Osgoode Hall Law School, York University, May 1984), 5.

79. Reinhold Kramer and Tom Mitchell, *When the State Trembled: How A.J. Andrews and the Citizens' Committee Broke the Winnipeg General Strike* (Toronto: University of Toronto Press, 2010), 248.

80. Fidler, 6.

81. Canada Criminal Code, section 98, subsection 6, in Fidler, appendix, 67.

82. Quoted in Fidler, 16–17.

83. Fidler, 23.

84. Ibid., 36.

85. Ibid., 37.

86. Ibid., 40.

87. W.H. Bullock-Webster to the Commissioner, B.C. Police, 27 September 1932: quoted in Endicott, 153–54.

88. Statement of Harold Hayes, President of the Mine Workers Union of Canada, 20 December 1933: Evans Fonds.

89. Fidler, 46. He notes, quoting the *Canadian Annual Review*, that the Saskatchewan Attorney General "decided that there was not enough evidence to warrant proceeding with the charges."

90. Ibid., 47.

91. Canada, House of Commons *Debates* (14 February 1933), Mr. Hugh Guthrie, MP.

CHAPTER 7: THE SPRING OF DISCONTENT

92. *Princeton Star*, 6 April 1933.
93. Ibid., 20 April 1933.
94. A photo of this "tombstone" appears in *Princeton Our Valley* (Princeton: Princeton History Book Committee, 2000), and the original is in the Burr fonds at the Princeton & District Museum & Archives.
95. The Zinoviev letter—one of the greatest British political scandals of the twentieth century—was supposedly from the Communist International to the Communist Party of Great Britain, and advocated accelerating the radicalization of the British working class by resuming diplomatic relations between the Communists and the sitting Labour government. It was forged by an MI6 agent's source and almost certainly leaked by MI6 or MI5 officers to the Conservative Party, and published in the *Daily Mail* four days before the British election of 1924, which Labour lost.
96. Taylor notes that "A facsimile reproduction appears in the *Sunday Dispatch* of 12 March, under the appropriate caption, 'By Order of the Soviet.'"
97. *Princeton Star*, 27 April 1933.
98. Ibid., 13 April 1933.
99. Ibid.
100. Ibid.
101. Endicott, 110.
102. "Wagontongue" refers to W.A. Wagenhauser, a local merchant and vice president of the board of trade (see photo on page 52). H.C. McGuffie was proprietor of the Princeton Cash Store, and sat on the board of trade council. John G. Biggs, the B.C. mine inspector, was widely thought by the miners to be in cahoots with the Tulameen management, and was also on the council. Dr. John R. Naden "treated" Beronich following his beating at the Brown Bridge, was in both kidnapping parties, and was on the council. Rev. John Goodfellow was a United Church minister, the first historian of Princeton and the surrounding district, and on both the board of Ttade council and the executive of the Citizens' League.
103. Evans Fonds.

CHAPTER 8: THE KIDNAPPING

104. There is nowhere a list of this "Executive," neither in the

newspaper nor in the Dave Taylor Fonds at the Princeton and District Museum and Archives. Had there been a copy in the files of the board of trade, it would have been burnt in the 1945 fire that destroyed all the board's records.

105. *Princeton Star*, special edition, 2 May 1933.

106. Of those we've not already encountered: Hall was the president of Princeton Power & Light, and had been variously the superintendent of Princeton Waterworks Co., superintendent of Princeton Coal & Land Co., and served on the school board for twenty years. Ewart was the owner of the local hardware store. On the union side, the 1932 *Directory* describes Plecash as a taxi driver; Francis, "Holland" (sic), Lockhart, and Ryder as miners at Tulameen Coal Mine; and Hayes and Cherkosh as president and secretary of the union, respectively.

107. Presumably the miners had already voted once to reject the cut, probably by show-of-hands, the traditional way of union voting.

108. *Princeton Star*, special edition, 2 May 1933.

109. Statements of Richard Ward, Walter McIntosh, and William Gee: Evans fonds. It is interesting to note the alleged presence of the mines inspector (J.J. Biggs), the newspaper editor (Dave Taylor) and the local doctor (Dr. Naden) among the company.

110. Murray was a pugnacious character, if the following account from the Evans fonds is to be believed. George Murray and Steve Freeman visited Cherkosh in his cabin and Murray said, "You rat, you slandered me in Press." "Before I could answer him he grabbed me by the throat, choking me, I got away from him and went into the next room, he followed me and started beating me up striking me in face and head and body. George Murray threatened to kill me if he got a chance." (Statement of John Cherkosh, Secretary of the Mine Workers Union, 19 December 1933.)

111. Additional Statements from Walter McIntosh, William Britton, and Arthur Chisholm, Evans Fonds.

CHAPTER 9: THE TRIALS OF SLIM EVANS

112. Sheils and Swankey, 56.

113. The *Star* of 15 June 1933 had its own problems with the jury: "Among the twelve jurors thus selected, there were seven known 'reds' and Mr. Bullock-Webster, crown counsel, objected. Gordon Grant, C.L.D.L. defender made the most of the point to secure for Evans an extension of his liberty."

114. *Unemployed Worker*, 14 June 1933.

115. *Princeton Star*, 22 June 1933.

116. Ibid., 6 July 1933. Taylor noted that "it is unlikely that another magistrate will be found who will consider the case."

117. R.H. Pooley, Attorney-General, to D. Taylor, Secretary, Princeton Board of Trade, 26 July 1933: both letters in Burr Fonds.

118. Grainger, 86.

119. *Princeton Star*, 6 July 1933.

120. Ibid., 3 August 1933.

121. A dismissal of the charge allowed for charges to be laid again; an acquittal would have protected the accused from such action.

122. *Princeton Star*, 3 August 1933.

123. Evidence of Constable William Thomson, *Rex v. Arthur Herbert Evans*, 9. "Should I Ever Be a Soldier" is a Joe Hill song found on page ninety of the 1932 edition (likely the one Evans had) of the "Little Red Songbook" (a.k.a. *IWW Songs to Fan the Flames of Discontent*). Its last verse, which might well have appealed to the Princeton miners, runs

> *Why do they mount their gatling gun / A thousand miles from ocean, / Where hostile fleet could never run— / Ain't that a funny notion? / If you don't know the reason why / Just strike for better wages, / And then, my friends—if you don't die— / You'll sing this song for ages.*

124. Mr. Justice W.A. MacDonald's Charge to the Jury in *Rex v. Arthur Herbert Evans*.

125. *Princeton Star*, 28 September 1933.

126. Sheils and Swankey, 72.

CHAPTER 10: THE AFTERMATH

127. S.W. Jackman, *Portraits of the Premiers: An Informal History of British Columbia* (Sidney, B.C.: Gray's Publishing, 1969), 213.

128. Tupper won with 43 percent of the vote. The incumbent, W.A. Mackenzie, had won as a Conservative in 1928 with 55 percent, but in 1933, running as part of the Non-Partisan Independent Group, received only 34 percent. Frank Brown of the CCF was third with 18 percent.

129. *Annual Report of Minister of Mines for 1935*, p. G-25.

130. *Campaign Bulletin #1*, Evans fonds.

131. RCMP, "Secret Report No. 753: Weekly Summary Report on Revolutionary Organizations and Agitators in Canada," in *R.C.M.P. Security Bulletins: The Depression Years*, Part II, 1935, eds. Gregory S. Kealey & Reg Whitaker (St. John's: Canadian Committee on Labour History, 1995), 238.

132. Ibid., 30.

133. Ibid., 124

134. Five of these poems have been reprinted in Jon Bartlett and Rika Ruebsaat, *Dead Horse on the Tulameen: Settler Verse from BC's Similkameen Valley* (Princeton: Canadian Folk Workshop, 2011).

135. Mills, 121.

136. Sheils and Swankey, 283.

Bibliography

Archives

Arthur Evans Fonds. Special Collections, University of British Columbia

B.C. Attorney General, 1857–1966, Boxes 417–26, 880: GR-0419, B.C. Archives.

B.C. Attorney General, 1872–1937, 1950: reel B09324 and boxes 20, 21: GR-0429, B.C. Archives.

B.C. Magistrates' Court. 1933. *Rex v. Gregory et al.* Coalmont.

B.C. Supreme Court. 1933. *Rex v. Arthur Herbert Evans*. Adjourned Spring Assizes, Vernon.

Burr Fonds. Princeton & District Museum & Archives

Dave Taylor Fonds. Princeton & District Museum & Archives.

Philip J. Thomas Song Collection. Aural History Archives, Royal B.C. Museum & Archives. Victoria, B.C.

Princeton County Court criminal case files 1925–39: GR-2504, B.C. Archives

RCMP Personal History File 175/P1072 [Arthur H. Evans].

Record of the Canadian Security Intelligence Service, RG 146, Vol 4670: Arthur Herbert Evans.

Government publications

B.C. Department of Labour. *Annual Report of the Department of Labour for the Year Ended December 31ˢᵗ 1932*. Victoria: British Columbia Legislative Assembly, 1932.

B.C. Supreme Court. 1933. *Rex v. Arthur Herbert Evans*. Adjourned Spring Assizes, Vernon.

Canada. 1891 Census of Canada. Library & Archives Canada. http://www.bac-lac.gc.ca/eng/census/1891/Pages/about-census.aspx.

Canada. *Forging Our Legacy: Canadian Citizenship and Immigration, 1900–1977*. Citizenship and Immigration Canada website: http://www.cic.gc.ca/english/resources/publications/legacy/chap-4b.asp#chap4-9.

Canada. House of Commons *Debates*. 14 February 1933.

Department of Mines. *Annual Report of the Minister of Mines of British Columbia*. Victoria: Legislative Assembly, 1925–1939.

F.E. Harrison. Preliminary Report to Deputy Minister of Labour. Ottawa, 15 December 1932.

NEWSPAPERS AND DIRECTORIES

B.C. *Directories*. 1890–1940.

Princeton Star. 1925–36.

Unemployed Worker. 1932–33.

Ubyssey (UBC Students' Union newspaper) 1924–26.

ARTICLES AND BOOKS

Angus, Ian. *Canadian Bolsheviks: The Early Years of the Communist Party of Canada*. Montreal: Vanguard Publications, 1981.

Bartlett, Jon, and Rika Ruebsaat. *Dead Horse on the Tulameen: Settler Verse from BC's Similkameen Valley*. Princeton: Canadian Folk Workshop, 2011.

Currie, Laurie. *Princeton 120 Years*. Princeton: Similkameen Spotlight Publishing, 1990.

Endicott, Stephen Lyon. *Raising the Workers' Flag: The Workers' Unity League of Canada, 1930-1936*. Toronto: University of Toronto Press, 2012.

Fidler, Richard. "Proscribing Unlawful Associations: The Swift Rise and Agonizing Demise of Section 98." Paper prepared for Professor Douglas Hay, Osgoode Hall Law School, York University, May 1984.

Goodfellow, John. *The Story of Similkameen*. Vol 1. Princeton: Princeton Centennial Committee, 1958.

Gorman, Louise Gwenyth. *State Control and Social Resistance: The Case of the Department of National Defence Relief Camp Scheme in B.C.* MA thesis, University of British Columbia, 1985.

Grainger, M. Allerdale. *Riding the Skyline*. Victoria, B.C.: Horsdal & Schubert, 1994.

Gray, James H. *The Winter Years*. Toronto: Macmillan of Canada, 1966.

Hoover, Herbert. *The Memoirs of Herbert Hoover*. Vol. 3, *The Great Depression*. London: Hollis and Carter, 1952.

IWW Songs to Fan the Flames of Discontent. 13th and 24th eds. Chicago: Industrial Workers of the World, 1917 and 1932.

Jackman, S.W. *Portraits of the Premiers: An Informal History of British Columbia*. Sidney, B.C.: Gray's Publishing, 1969.

Kealey, Gregory S., and Reg Whitaker, eds. *R.C.M.P. Security Bulletins: The Depression Years, Part I, 1933–1934*. St. John's: Canadian Committee on Labour History, 1993.

Kramer, Reinhold and Tom Mitchell, *When the State Trembled: How A.J. Andrews and the Citizens' Committee Broke the Winnipeg General Strike*. Toronto: University of Toronto Press, 2010.

Kyle, Franz. "One Flag, One School, One Language: The Ku Klux Klan and the Crowsnest Pass, 1932." In *Heritage News*, Issue 3, 15 July 2010.

LeFresne, G.M. "The Royal Twenty Centers: The Department of National Defence and Federal Unemployment Relief 1932–1936." Graduating Essay, Royal Military College of Canada, Kingston, 1962.

Mills, Nicholas. *Once Upon a Time in Princeton*. Chilliwack, B.C.: self-published, 2013.

Molinaro, Dennis G. "'A Species of Treason?': Deportation and Nation-Building in the Case of Tomo Čačić, 1931–1934." *Canadian Historical Review* 91, no. 1 (2010): 61–85.

Petryshyn, J. "Class Conflict and Civil Liberties: The Origins and Activities of the Canadian Labour Defense League, 1925-1940." *Labour/Le Travailleur* 10 (1982): 39–63.

Princeton History Committee. *Princeton, Our Valley*. Princeton: Princeton History Committee, 2000.

RCMP. "Secret Report No. 753: Weekly Summary Report on Revolutionary Organizations and Agitators in Canada." In *R.C.M.P. Security Bulletins: The Depression Years, Part II, 1935*, eds. Gregory S. Kealey and Reg Whitaker. St. John's: Canadian Committee on Labour History, 1995.

Seager, Allan. "A History of the Mine Workers Union of Canada." MA thesis, McGill University, Montreal, 1977.

Sheils, Jean Evans, and Ben Swankey. *Work and Wages! Semi-Documentary Account of the Life and Times of Arthur H. (Slim)*

Evans. Vancouver: Trade Union Research Bureau, 1977.

Sher, Julian. *White Hoods: Canada's Ku Klux Klan.* Vancouver: New Star Books, 1983.

Stonier-Newman, Lynne. *Policing a Pioneer Province: The BC Provincial Police 1858-1950.* Madeira Park, B.C.: Harbour Publishing, 1991.

Strikwerda, Eric. "'Married Men Should, I Feel, Be Treated Differently': Work, Relief, and Unemployed Men on the Urban Canadian Prairie, 1929–1932." *Left History* 12, no. 1 (2007): 30–51.

Photo Credits

Cover; pp. iii and 60: *Unity*, courtesy of UBC Library's Rare Books and Special Collections.

p. 20: *Princeton Star*, courtesy of Princeton and District Museum and Archives.

p. 24: Princeton and District Museum and Archives.

p. 31: *Unemployed Worker*, courtesy of B.C. Archives microfilm.

p. 34 (top): Library and Archives Canada, HPMP 050.

p. 34 (bottom): Canada. Dept. of National Defence / Library and Archives Canada / PA–035142.

p. 39 (top): Library and Archives Canada, HPMP 024C.

p. 39 (bottom): Canada. Dept. of National Defence / Library and Archives Canada / PA–035147.

p. 43: *Pacific Tribune* collection, courtesy of B.C. Labour History Centre.

p. 52: Princeton and District Museum and Archives, Personalities, Unknown #7.

p. 65: Princeton & District Museum & Archives, Burr Fonds.

p. 68: Image G-05174, courtesy of the Royal B.C. Museum and Archives.

p. 72: *Princeton Star*, Princeton and District Museum and Archives.

p. 79: *Princeton Star*, Princeton and District Museum and Archives.

p. 87: *Unemployed Worker*, B.C. Archives microfilm.

p. 90: Courtesy of Glenbow Archives, Calgary, NA–3634–2.

Index